BEGINN SPANISH DICTIONARY

Helen Davies
Illustrated by John Shackell
Designed by Brian Robertson
Edited by Nicole Irving

Language consultants: Jane Straker and Gloria Brass
Handlettering by Jack Potter
Additional designs by Kim Blundell
Editorial help from Anita Ganeri

Contents

Using this book

This book contains over 2,000 useful Spanish words, with pictures to help you remember them. To help you identify words, nouns (naming words) are printed in roman lettering (*el libro*, book) and verbs (doing words), adjectives (describing words) and phrases in italics (*grande*, big).

Nouns

Spanish nouns are either masculine or feminine (this is called their gender). The Spanish word for "the" shows which gender a noun is. "The" is **el** when the word is masculine and **la** when it is feminine. In the plural **el** becomes **los** and **la** becomes **las.** Sometimes the following abbreviations are also used: **(f)** feminine, **(m)** masculine, **(s)** singular and **(pl)** plural.

In Spanish, nouns that describe what people do or what they are (e.g. dancer) often have a masculine and a feminine form. When they appear in the illustrated section of the book only the form which matches the picture is given, but both masculine and feminine forms are given in the alphabetical word list at the back.

Spanish words often have a mark over one of the vowels (e.g. **el balcón**). This is called a stress mark and shows that you should emphasize that part of the word. You can find out more about pronouncing Spanish words at the beginning of the word list on page 109.

Adjectives

Adjectives in Spanish change their ending depending on whether the noun they are describing is masculine or feminine. Most adjectives end in **o** in the masculine and the **o** changes to **a** in the feminine.

In the pictures the adjective matches the noun illustrated. However it is useful to learn both masculine and feminine forms, so both are given in the word box. When you see only one form, it means the masculine and feminine are the same.

Verbs

Throughout the book verbs appear in the infinitive ("to hide, to look for" in English). In Spanish, infinitives end in either **ar, er** or **ir.** You can find out how to use verbs on page 98 and there is a list of irregular verbs on page 103.

el bailarín

flaca

buscar

3

Meeting people

¡Hola! — Hello
¡Adiós! — Goodbye
¡Hasta pronto!* — See you later.
dar la mano — to shake hands
dar un beso — to kiss

el hombre — man
la mujer — woman
el bebé — baby
el niño — boy
la niña — girl

presentar — to introduce
la amiga — friend (f)
el amigo — friend (m)
encontrarse con — to meet

¿Qué tal? — How are you?
Muy bien, ¡gracias! — Very well, thank you.

*You can find the literal meaning of phrases and expressions in the Phrase explainer section on pages 106-9.

charlar	to chat
Sí	Yes
No	No
De acuerdo.	I agree.
decir	to say
echarse a reír	to burst out laughing

charlar

Sí

No

De acuerdo.

decir

echarse a reír

el nombre

el nombre de pila
Pilar RUÍZ

el apellido

el nombre	name
el nombre de pila	first name
el apellido	surname
¿Cómo te llamas?	What's your name?
Me llamo...	My name is…
El se llama...	His name is…

Me llamo...

El se llama...

¿Cómo te llamas?

la edad

¿Cuántos años tienes?

pequeño

mayor que

más pequeño que

mayor

Tengo diecinueve años.

la misma edad

la edad	age	mayor	old
¿Cuántos años tienes?	How old are you?	**mayor que**	older than
Tengo diecinueve años.	I'm nineteen.	**más pequeño(a) que**	younger than
pequeño(a)	young	**la misma edad**	the same age

5

Families

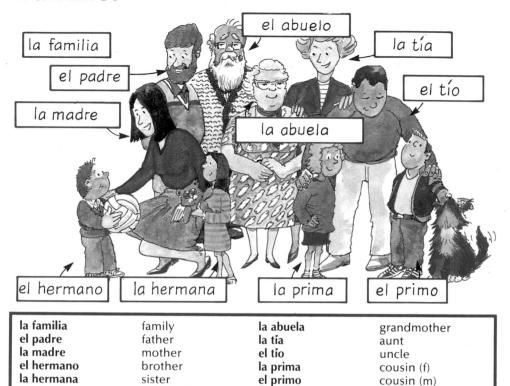

el abuelo

la familia

el padre

la madre

la tía

el tío

la abuela

el hermano | la hermana | la prima | el primo

la familia	family	la abuela	grandmother
el padre	father	la tía	aunt
la madre	mother	el tío	uncle
el hermano	brother	la prima	cousin (f)
la hermana	sister	el primo	cousin (m)
el abuelo	grandfather		

ser parientes

el hijo

el nieto

la hija

la nieta

el sobrino

criar | tenerle cariño a | la sobrina

ser parientes	to be related	la nieta	granddaughter
el hijo	son	tenerle cariño a	to be fond of
la hija	daughter	el sobrino	nephew
criar	to bring up	la sobrina	niece
el nieto	grandson		

la mujer	wife
el marido	husband
los padres	parents
querer a	to love
los hijos	children
los gemelos	twin brothers
el hijo único	only son

la mujer

el marido

los padres

querer a

los hijos

los gemelos

el hijo único

la vida

la niñez

el casamiento

el nacimiento

nacer

casarse

la boda

la muerte

trabajar

la vejez

morirse

el entierro

la vida	life	**la boda**	wedding
el nacimiento	birth	**trabajar**	to work
nacer	to be born	**la vejez**	old age
la niñez	childhood	**la muerte**	death
el casamiento	marriage	**morirse**	to die
casarse	to get married	**el entierro**	funeral

Appearance and personality

bonita

guapo

fuerte

flaco

débil

delgada

gordo

bonito(a)	pretty
guapo(a)	handsome
fuerte	strong
débil	weak
flaco(a)	thin
delgado(a)	slim
gordo(a)	fat

tener el pelo rubio

ser calvo

... el pelo castaño

... el pelo rojo

... el pelo laso

... el pelo rizado

... flequillo

... trenzas

tener el pelo rubio	to have blond hair	el pelo rizado	curly hair
el pelo castaño	brown hair	flequillo	bangs
el pelo rojo	red hair	trenzas	braids
el pelo laso	straight hair	ser calvo	to be bald

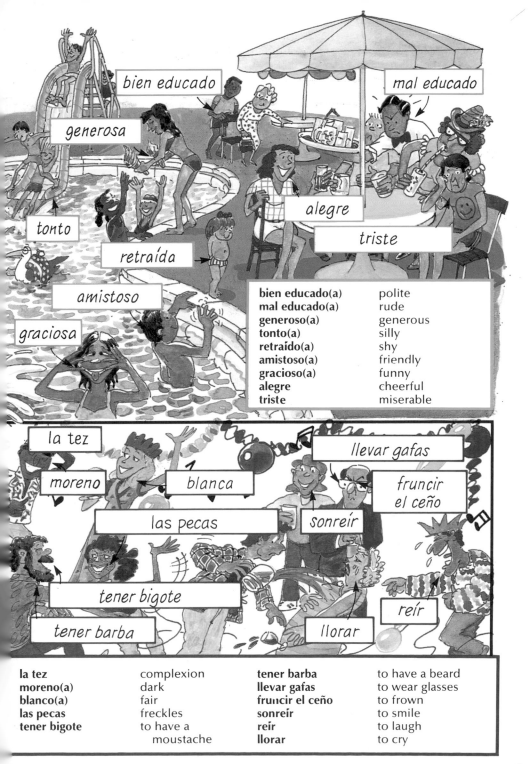

bien educado

mal educado

generosa

alegre

tonto

triste

retraída

amistoso

graciosa

bien educado(a)	polite
mal educado(a)	rude
generoso(a)	generous
tonto(a)	silly
retraído(a)	shy
amistoso(a)	friendly
gracioso(a)	funny
alegre	cheerful
triste	miserable

la tez

llevar gafas

moreno

blanca

fruncir el ceño

las pecas

sonreír

tener bigote

reír

tener barba

llorar

la tez	complexion	**tener barba**	to have a beard
moreno(a)	dark	**llevar gafas**	to wear glasses
blanco(a)	fair	**fruncir el ceño**	to frown
las pecas	freckles	**sonreír**	to smile
tener bigote	to have a moustache	**reír**	to laugh
		llorar	to cry

Your body

la cabeza	head
el pelo	hair
la cara	face
la piel	skin
el ojo	eye
la mejilla	cheek
la nariz	nose
la oreja	ear
la boca	mouth
el diente	tooth
la lengua	tongue
el labio	lip
el cuello	neck
la barbilla	chin

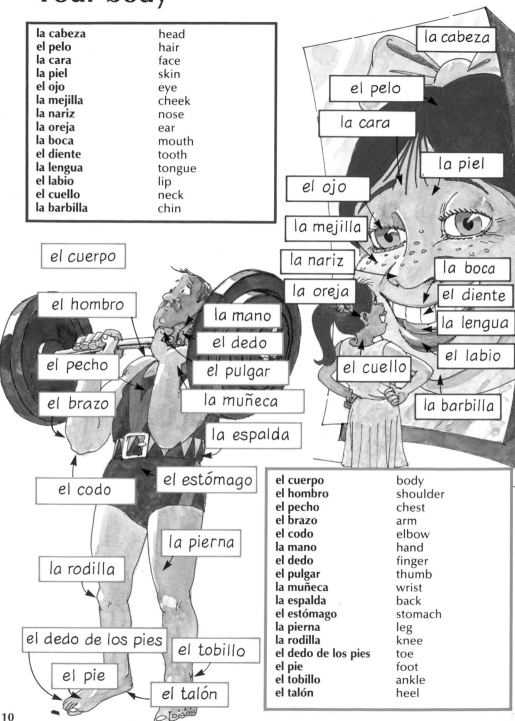

la cabeza

el pelo

la cara

la piel

el ojo

la mejilla

la nariz

la oreja

la boca

el diente

la lengua

el labio

el cuerpo

el hombro

la mano

el dedo

el pulgar

el pecho

el cuello

el brazo

la muñeca

la barbilla

la espalda

el codo

el estómago

la pierna

la rodilla

el dedo de los pies

el tobillo

el pie

el talón

el cuerpo	body
el hombro	shoulder
el pecho	chest
el brazo	arm
el codo	elbow
la mano	hand
el dedo	finger
el pulgar	thumb
la muñeca	wrist
la espalda	back
el estómago	stomach
la pierna	leg
la rodilla	knee
el dedo de los pies	toe
el pie	foot
el tobillo	ankle
el talón	heel

ser alto(a)	to be tall
ser bajo(a)	to be short
pesarse	to weigh yourself
ser ligero(a)	to be light
ser pesado(a)	to be heavy

ser alto

ser bajo

pesarse

ser ligero

ser pesado

el lado izquierdo

el lado derecho

el lado izquierdo	left side
el lado derecho	right side

arrodillarse

tumbarse

estar echado

andar descalzo

estar de rodillas

sentarse

ponerse de pie

estar de pie

estar sentada

andar descalzo(a)	to walk barefoot
ponerse de pie	to stand up
estar de pie	to be standing
arrodillarse	to kneel down
estar de rodillas	to be kneeling
tumbarse	to lie down
estar echado(a)	to be lying down
sentarse	to sit down
estar sentado(a)	to be sitting down

Houses and homes

la casa de pisos

el piso

Es mi casa.

segundo piso

la puerta de entrada

la casa de pisos	block of apartments
el piso	apartment
Es mi casa.	This is where I live.
segundo piso(m)	second floor
la puerta de entrada	front door
el timbre	doorbell
tocar el timbre	to ring the bell
el buzón	letter box
el felpudo	doormat
el balcón	balcony
primer piso	first floor
el portero	caretaker (m)
venirse a vivir	to move in
piso bajo	ground floor

el timbre

tocar el timbre

el buzón

el felpudo

el balcón

el portero

venirse a vivir

piso bajo

la casa

vivir en una casa

la vecina

la patrona

mudarse

primer piso

el huésped

el sótano

la casa	house
vivir en una casa	to live in a house
la vecina	neighbor (f)
la patrona	landlady
mudarse	to move out
el huésped	tenant (m/f)
el sótano	basement

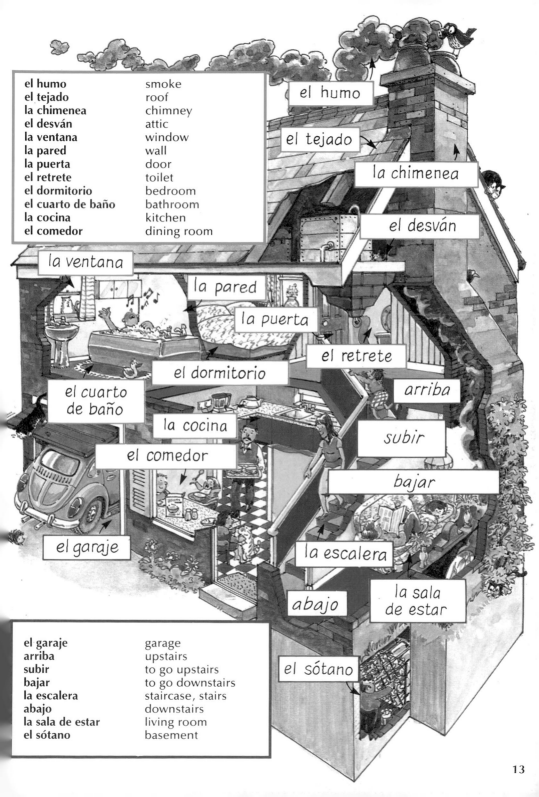

el humo	smoke
el tejado	roof
la chimenea	chimney
el desván	attic
la ventana	window
la pared	wall
la puerta	door
el retrete	toilet
el dormitorio	bedroom
el cuarto de baño	bathroom
la cocina	kitchen
el comedor	dining room

el humo

el tejado

la chimenea

el desván

la ventana

la pared

la puerta

el retrete

el dormitorio

arriba

el cuarto de baño

subir

la cocina

el comedor

bajar

el garaje

la escalera

abajo

la sala de estar

el sótano

el garaje	garage
arriba	upstairs
subir	to go upstairs
bajar	to go downstairs
la escalera	staircase, stairs
abajo	downstairs
la sala de estar	living room
el sótano	basement

Dining room and living room

el comedor	dining room
la luz	light
el radiador	radiator
la mesa	table
la silla	chair
el suelo	floor
la alfombra	carpet, rug

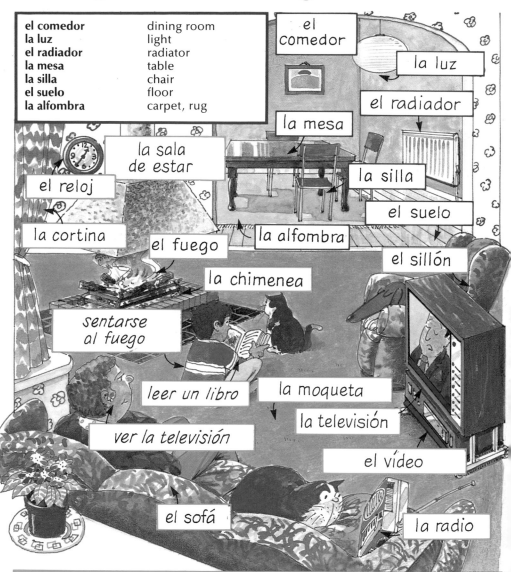

el comedor

la luz

el radiador

la mesa

la silla

el suelo

la sala de estar

el reloj

la cortina

el fuego

la chimenea

la alfombra

el sillón

sentarse al fuego

leer un libro

la moqueta

la televisión

ver la televisión

el vídeo

el sofá

la radio

la sala de estar	living room	**ver la televisión**	to watch television
el reloj	clock	**el sofá**	sofa
la cortina	curtain	**la moqueta**	wall-to-wall carpet
el fuego	fire	**la televisión**	television
la chimenea	fireplace	**el video**	VCR (video cassette recorder)
el sillón	armchair		
sentarse al fuego	to sit by the fire	**la radio**	radio
leer un libro	to read a book		

In the kitchen

la cocina

la alacena

la lavadora

lavar la ropa

la nevera

el horno

guisar

la cacerola

planchar

el gas

la lata de la basura

secar

el enchufe

la electricidad

el paño de cocina

pasar la aspiradora

fregar

limpio

sucia

el fregadero

la cocina	kitchen
la alacena	cupboard
la lavadora	washing machine
lavar la ropa	to do the washing
la nevera	fridge

el horno	oven	**pasar la aspiradora**	to vacuum
guisar	to cook	**fregar**	to do the dishes
la cacerola	saucepan	**sucio(a)**	dirty
el gas	gas	**el fregadero**	sink
la lata de la basura	waste basket	**secar**	to dry
planchar	to iron	**el paño de cocina**	tea towel
el enchufe	plug	**limpio(a)**	clean
la electricidad	electricity		

In the garden

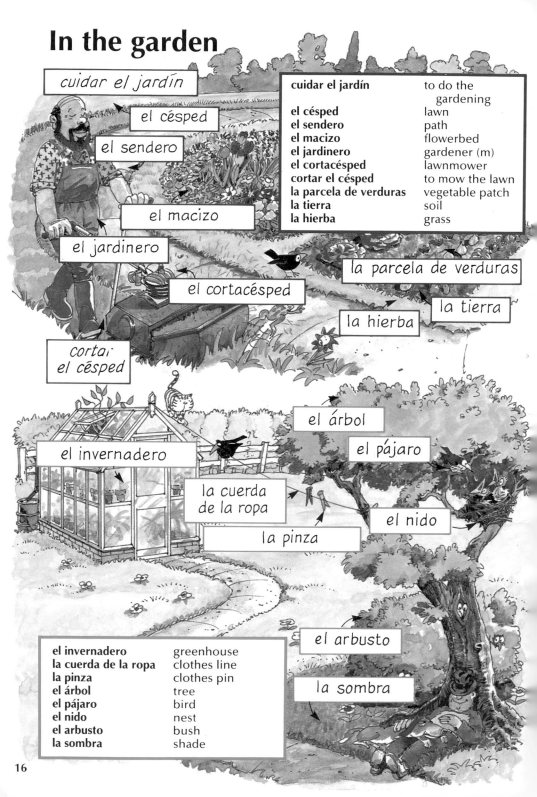

cuidar el jardín

el césped

el sendero

el macizo

el jardinero

el cortacésped

cortar el césped

la parcela de verduras

la tierra

la hierba

cuidar el jardín	to do the gardening
el césped	lawn
el sendero	path
el macizo	flowerbed
el jardinero	gardener (m)
el cortacésped	lawnmower
cortar el césped	to mow the lawn
la parcela de verduras	vegetable patch
la tierra	soil
la hierba	grass

el árbol

el pájaro

el invernadero

la cuerda de la ropa

el nido

la pinza

el arbusto

la sombra

el invernadero	greenhouse
la cuerda de la ropa	clothes line
la pinza	clothes pin
el árbol	tree
el pájaro	bird
el nido	nest
el arbusto	bush
la sombra	shade

la abeja	bee	**el tulipán**	tulip
la mariposa	butterfly	**la nomeolvides**	forget-me-not
la avispa	wasp	**el clavel**	carnation
picar	to sting	**las semillas**	seeds
la rosa	rose	**plantar**	to plant
oler bien	to smell sweet	**el bulbo**	bulb
bonito(a)	pretty, lovely	**quitar los hierbajos**	to weed
el crisantemo	chrysanthemum	**el hierbajo**	weed
el geraneo	geranium		

la caseta de jardín	garden shed
la carretilla	wheelbarrow
el desplantador	trowel
el rastrillo	rake
la pala	spade
la horquilla	fork
la regadera	watering can

Pets

el perro	dog
la perrera	kennel
el cachorro	puppy
el pelo	fur
la pata	paw
juguetón	playful
ladrar	to bark
¡ATENCION AL PERRO!	BEWARE OF THE DOG
perseguir	to chase
traer	to fetch
el rabo	tail
mover el rabo	to wag its tail
gruñir	to growl
sacar a paseo	to take for a walk

el perro

la perrera

el cachorro

el pelo

la pata

juguetón

ladrar

¡ATENCION AL PERRO!

perseguir

gruñir

traer

el rabo

mover el rabo

sacar a paseo

el gato	cat
el cesto	basket
ronronear	to purr
el gatito	kitten
maullar	to mew
estirar	to stretch
la garra	claw
suave	soft
encantador(a)	sweet

el gato

el cesto

ronronear

el gatito

maullar

estirar

la garra

suave

encantador

el canario	canary	el conejo	rabbit
posarse	to perch	la tortuga	turtle
el ala	wing	la jaula	cage
el pico	beak	dar de comer	to feed
la pluma	feather	el pez de colores	goldfish
el hámster	hamster	el ratón	mouse
el erizo	hedgehog	el cuenco de cristal	bowl
el conejillo de Indias	guinea pig		

Getting up

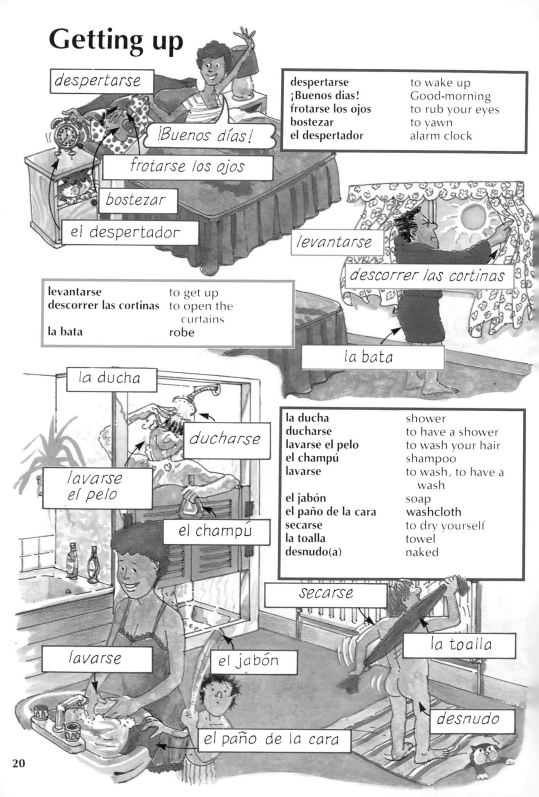

despertarse

¡Buenos días!

frotarse los ojos

bostezar

el despertador

despertarse	to wake up
¡Buenos dias!	Good-morning
frotarse los ojos	to rub your eyes
bostezar	to yawn
el despertador	alarm clock

levantarse

descorrer las cortinas

levantarse	to get up
descorrer las cortinas	to open the curtains
la bata	robe

la bata

la ducha

ducharse

lavarse el pelo

el champú

la ducha	shower
ducharse	to have a shower
lavarse el pelo	to wash your hair
el champú	shampoo
lavarse	to wash, to have a wash
el jabón	soap
el paño de la cara	washcloth
secarse	to dry yourself
la toalla	towel
desnudo(a)	naked

secarse

la toalla

lavarse

el jabón

desnudo

el paño de la cara

afeitarse	to shave
el espejo	mirror
la afeitadora eléctrica	electric shaver
la maquinilla de afeitar	razor
la espuma de afeitar	shaving foam

afeitarse

el espejo

la afeitadora eléctrica

la maquinilla de afeitar

la espuma de afeitar

el agua caliente

el agua fría

el grifo

la pasta de dientes

el cepillo de dientes

limpiarse los dientes

el grifo	tap
el agua(f)* caliente	hot water
el agua fría	cold water
la pasta de dientes	toothpaste
el cepillo de dientes	toothbrush
limpiarse los dientes	to clean your teeth

secarse el pelo	to dry your hair
la secadora eléctrica	hairdrier
el cepillo	brush
el peine	comb
peinarse	to comb your hair
cepillarse el pelo	to brush your hair

secarse el pelo

la secadora eléctrica

el cepillo

el peine

maquillarse

el rímel

la crema base

peinarse

cepillarse el pelo

la barra de labios

el perfume

maquillarse	to put on make-up
el rímel	mascara
la crema base	foundation cream
la barra de labios	lipstick
el perfume	perfume

*You say **el agua** even though it's feminine. This is because **el** is sometimes used instead of **la** in front of nouns beginning with "a" or "ha".

Clothes

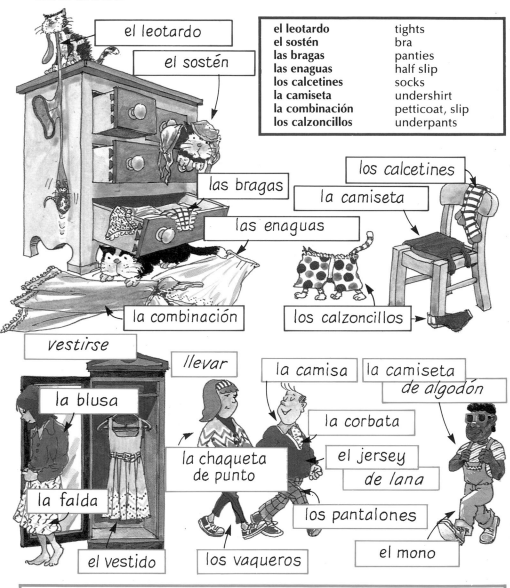

el leotardo

el sostén

el leotardo	tights
el sostén	bra
las bragas	panties
las enaguas	half slip
los calcetines	socks
la camiseta	undershirt
la combinación	petticoat, slip
los calzoncillos	underpants

las bragas

los calcetines

la camiseta

las enaguas

la combinación

los calzoncillos

vestirse

llevar

la camisa

la camiseta de algodón

la blusa

la corbata

la chaqueta de punto

el jersey de lana

la falda

los pantalones

el vestido

los vaqueros

el mono

vestirse	to get dressed	**la corbata**	tie
la blusa	blouse	**el jersey**	sweater
la falda	skirt	**de lana**	woollen
el vestido	dress	**los pantalones**	trousers
llevar	to wear	**la camiseta**	T-shirt
la chaqueta de punto	cardigan	**de algodón**	cotton, made of cotton
los vaqueros	jeans		
la camisa	shirt	**el mono**	dungarees

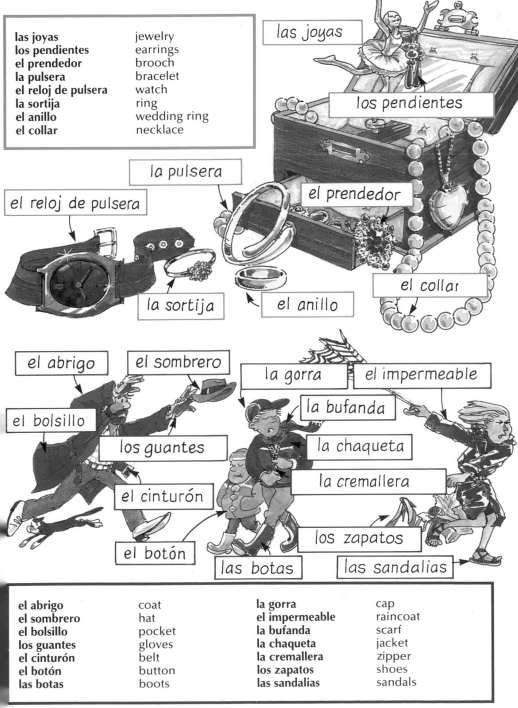

las joyas	jewelry
los pendientes	earrings
el prendedor	brooch
la pulsera	bracelet
el reloj de pulsera	watch
la sortija	ring
el anillo	wedding ring
el collar	necklace

las joyas

los pendientes

la pulsera

el reloj de pulsera

el prendedor

el collar

la sortija

el anillo

el abrigo

el sombrero

la gorra

el impermeable

el bolsillo

la bufanda

los guantes

la chaqueta

el cinturón

la cremallera

el botón

los zapatos

las botas

las sandalias

el abrigo	coat	**la gorra**	cap
el sombrero	hat	**el impermeable**	raincoat
el bolsillo	pocket	**la bufanda**	scarf
los guantes	gloves	**la chaqueta**	jacket
el cinturón	belt	**la cremallera**	zipper
el botón	button	**los zapatos**	shoes
las botas	boots	**las sandalias**	sandals

Going to bed

la hora de acostarse	bedtime
encender la luz	to switch the light on
estar cansado(a)	to be sleepy
poner orden	to tidy up
quitarse la ropa	to get undressed

la hora de acostarse

encender la luz

estar cansada

poner orden

quitarse la ropa

poner el baño

bañarse

el baño

el tapón de baño

salpicar

el albornoz

la esterita de baño

la báscula

poner el baño	to run the bath
bañarse	to have a bath
el baño	bathtub
el tapón de baño	plug
el albornoz	bathrobe
salpicar	to splash
la esterita de baño	bathmat
la báscula	scales

acostarse

el pijama

el camisón

las zapatillas

acostarse	to go to bed
el pijama	pajamas
el camisón	nightgown
las zapatillas	slippers

la canción de cuna

leer un cuento

la cuna

dormirse

la canción de cuna	lullaby
leer un cuento	to read a story
la cuna	crib
dormirse	to fall asleep

¡Hasta mañana!

¡Qué duermas bien!

soñar

roncar

dormir

la almohada

apagar

la lámpara

la sábana

el duvé

la colcha

la mesilla de noche

la cama

¡Hasta mañana!	Good-night.	**la mesilla de noche**	bedside table
¡Qué duermas bien!	Sleep well.	**el duvé**	quilt
soñar	to dream	**la cama**	bed
dormir	to sleep	**roncar**	to snore
apagar	to switch the light off	**la almohada**	pillow
		la sábana	sheet
la lámpara	lamp	**la colcha**	bedspread

Eating and drinking

poner la mesa	to set the table
Ya está.	It's ready.
la cafetera	coffee-pot
la tetera	teapot
la servilleta	napkin
el vaso	glass
el tazón	bowl
el plato	plate
la taza	cup
el platillo	saucer
el mantel	tablecloth
el jarro	pitcher
la cuchara	spoon
el cuchillo	knife
el tenedor	fork

poner la mesa

Ya está.

la cafetera

la tetera

la servilleta

el vaso

la taza

la cuchara

el platillo

el cuchillo

el tazón

el plato

el jarro

el tenedor

el mantel

¡Sírvete!

¡Qué aproveche!

tener hambre

tener sed

comer

beber

Está muy rico.

haber comido bien

¡Sírvete!	Help yourself.
¡Qué aproveche!	Enjoy your meal.
tener sed	to be thirsty
beber	to drink
tener hambre	to be hungry
comer	to eat
Está muy rico.	It tastes good.
haber comido bien	to have eaten well

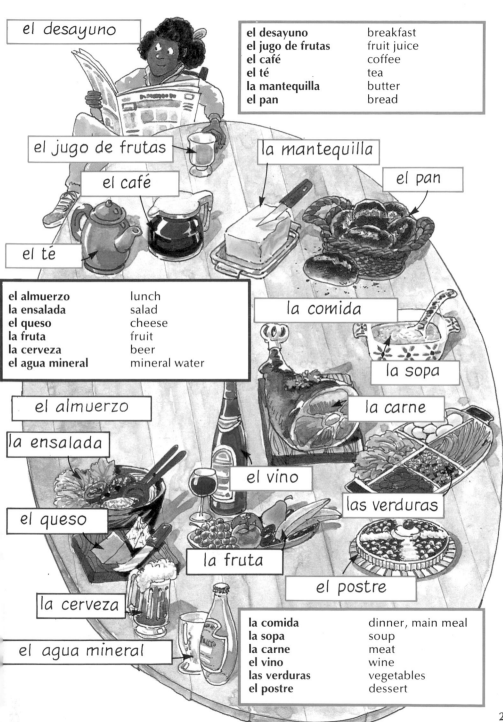

el desayuno

el desayuno	breakfast
el jugo de frutas	fruit juice
el café	coffee
el té	tea
la mantequilla	butter
el pan	bread

el jugo de frutas

la mantequilla

el café

el pan

el té

el almuerzo	lunch
la ensalada	salad
el queso	cheese
la fruta	fruit
la cerveza	beer
el agua mineral	mineral water

la comida

la sopa

el almuerzo

la carne

la ensalada

el vino

el queso

las verduras

la fruta

el postre

la cerveza

la comida	dinner, main meal
la sopa	soup
la carne	meat
el vino	wine
las verduras	vegetables
el postre	dessert

el agua mineral

Buying food

la carne

el chorizo

el salchichón

la pierna de cordero

la chuleta de cerdo

el filete

el pollo

el jamón

la ternera

la salchicha

el guisante

las verduras

fresco

la zanahoria

la ensalada

crudo

las espinacas

la col

el tomate

el ajo

la coliflor

la judía verde

la cebolla

la col de Bruselas

la patata

la carne	meat		
el chorizo	spicy cooked sausage		
el salchichón	salami		
la pierna de cordero	leg of lamb		
la chuleta de cerdo	pork chop		
el pollo	chicken		
el filete	steak		
el jamón	ham		
la ternera	veal		
la salchicha	sausage		

las verduras	vegetables	**la coliflor**	cauliflower
fresco(a)	fresh	**la col de Bruselas**	Brussels sprout
la col	cabbage	**la ensalada**	salad
el ajo	garlic	**crudo(a)**	raw
la cebolla	onion	**el tomate**	tomato
el guisante	pea	**la judía verde**	green bean
la zanahoria	carrot	**la patata**	potato
las espinacas	spinach		

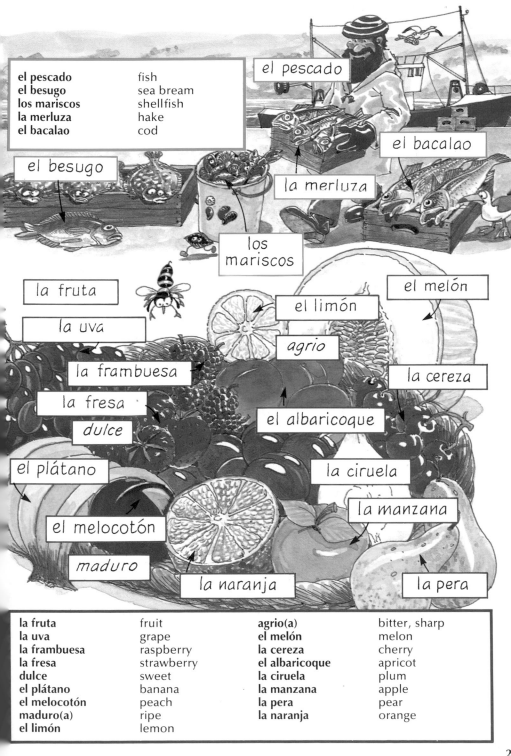

el pescado	fish
el besugo	sea bream
los mariscos	shellfish
la merluza	hake
el bacalao	cod

el pescado

el bacalao

la merluza

el besugo

los mariscos

la fruta

la uva

el melón

el limón

agrio

la frambuesa

la cereza

la fresa

el albaricoque

dulce

el plátano

la ciruela

la manzana

el melocotón

maduro

la naranja

la pera

la fruta	fruit	agrio(a)	bitter, sharp
la uva	grape	el melón	melon
la frambuesa	raspberry	la cereza	cherry
la fresa	strawberry	el albaricoque	apricot
dulce	sweet	la ciruela	plum
el plátano	banana	la manzana	apple
el melocotón	peach	la pera	pear
maduro(a)	ripe	la naranja	orange
el limón	lemon		

Buying food

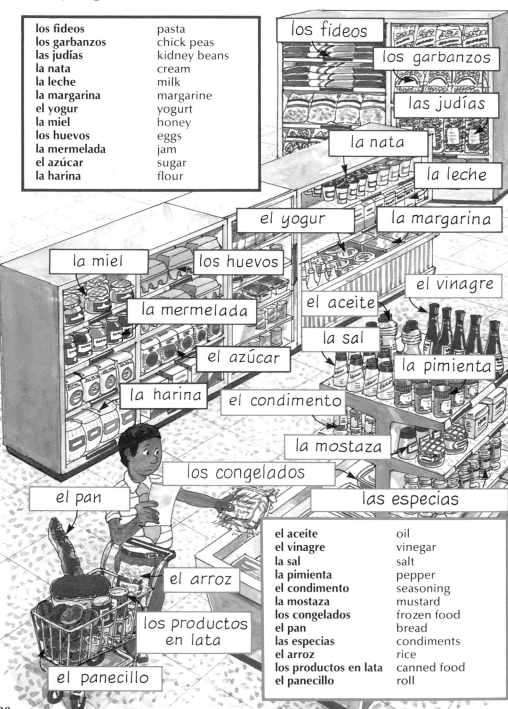

los fideos	pasta
los garbanzos	chick peas
las judías	kidney beans
la nata	cream
la leche	milk
la margarina	margarine
el yogur	yogurt
la miel	honey
los huevos	eggs
la mermelada	jam
el azúcar	sugar
la harina	flour

los fideos

los garbanzos

las judías

la nata

la leche

el yogur

la margarina

la miel

los huevos

el vinagre

el aceite

la mermelada

la sal

el azúcar

la pimienta

la harina

el condimento

la mostaza

los congelados

las especias

el pan

el arroz

los productos en lata

el panecillo

el aceite	oil
el vinagre	vinegar
la sal	salt
la pimienta	pepper
el condimento	seasoning
la mostaza	mustard
los congelados	frozen food
el pan	bread
las especias	condiments
el arroz	rice
los productos en lata	canned food
el panecillo	roll

el chocolate	chocolate
la galleta	cookie
la tarta	tart
el buñuelo	doughnut
la torta	cake
el helado	ice-cream
el pastel	pastry, small tart

el chocolate

la galleta

la tarta

el buñuelo

la torta

el pastel

el helado

guisar

la receta

probar

el sabor

el ingrediente

mezclar

¡Riquísimo!

guisar	to cook
la receta	recipe
el ingrediente	ingredient
mezclar	to mix
probar	to taste
el sabor	flavor, taste
¡Riquísimo!	Delicious!

31

Pastimes

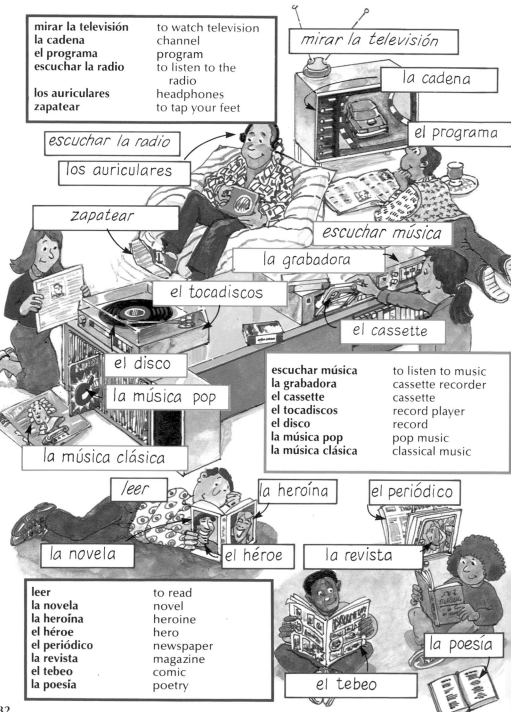

mirar la televisión	to watch television
la cadena	channel
el programa	program
escuchar la radio	to listen to the radio
los auriculares	headphones
zapatear	to tap your feet

mirar la televisión

la cadena

el programa

escuchar la radio

los auriculares

zapatear

escuchar música

la grabadora

el tocadiscos

el cassette

el disco

la música pop

la música clásica

escuchar música	to listen to music
la grabadora	cassette recorder
el cassette	cassette
el tocadiscos	record player
el disco	record
la música pop	pop music
la música clásica	classical music

leer

la heroína

el periódico

la novela

el héroe

la revista

la poesía

el tebeo

leer	to read
la novela	novel
la heroína	heroine
el héroe	hero
el periódico	newspaper
la revista	magazine
el tebeo	comic
la poesía	poetry

hacer punto

las agujas

el patrón

hacer punto	to knit
las agujas	knitting needles
el patrón	pattern
la lana	yarn

la lana

coser

coser	to sew
la tela	fabric
las tijeras	scissors
el hilo	thread
el alfiler	pin
la aguja	needle
la cinta elástica	elastic

la tela

el hilo

la cinta elástica

la aguja

las tijeras

el alfiler

la carpintería

hábil

el martillo

reparar

el tornillo

el atornillador

la sierra

hacer

la carpintería	woodwork
hábil	skillful, good with your hands
la sierra	saw
hacer	to make
el martillo	hammer
reparar	to mend
el tornillo	screw
el atornillador	screwdriver

33

Pastimes

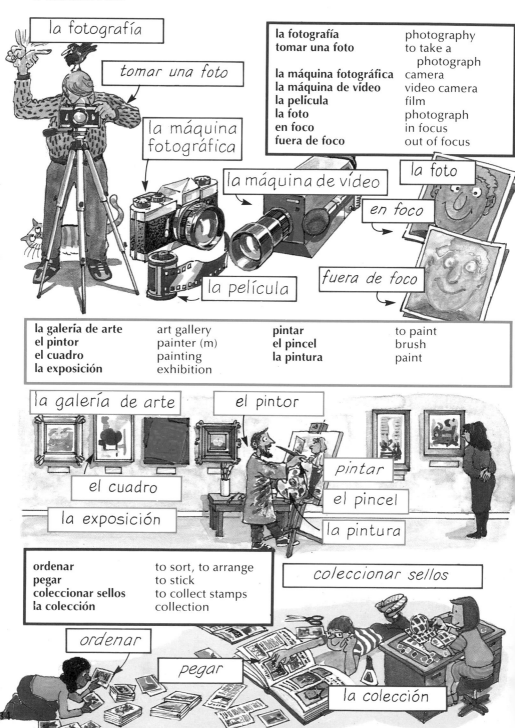

la fotografía

tomar una foto

la máquina fotográfica

la fotografía	photography
tomar una foto	to take a photograph
la máquina fotográfica	camera
la máquina de vídeo	video camera
la película	film
la foto	photograph
en foco	in focus
fuera de foco	out of focus

la máquina de vídeo

la foto

en foco

fuera de foco

la película

la galería de arte	art gallery	**pintar**	to paint
el pintor	painter (m)	**el pincel**	brush
el cuadro	painting	**la pintura**	paint
la exposición	exhibition		

la galería de arte

el pintor

el cuadro

la exposición

pintar

el pincel

la pintura

ordenar	to sort, to arrange
pegar	to stick
coleccionar sellos	to collect stamps
la colección	collection

coleccionar sellos

ordenar

pegar

la colección

la músico	musician (f)	**tocar los tambores**	to play the drums
el instrumento	instrument	**tocar la trompeta**	to play the trumpet
tocar el violín	to play the violin	**tocar el violoncelo**	to play the cello
tocar el piano	to play the piano	**la orquesta**	orchestra
tocar la guitarra	to play the guitar	**el director de orquesta**	conductor (m)

la músico

el instrumento

tocar el piano

tocar el violín

tocar la guitarra

tocar los tambores

tocar la trompeta

tocar el violoncelo

la orquesta

el director de orquesta

cantar

la melodía

cantar	to sing
la melodía	tune
el coro	choir
cantar desafinado	to sing out of tune

cantar desafinado

el coro

los juegos

jugar a las cartas

jugar a las damas

los juegos	games
jugar a las cartas	to play cards
jugar a las damas	to play checkers
jugar al ajedrez	to play chess
los juegos de tablero	board games

los juegos de tablero

jugar al ajedrez

Going out

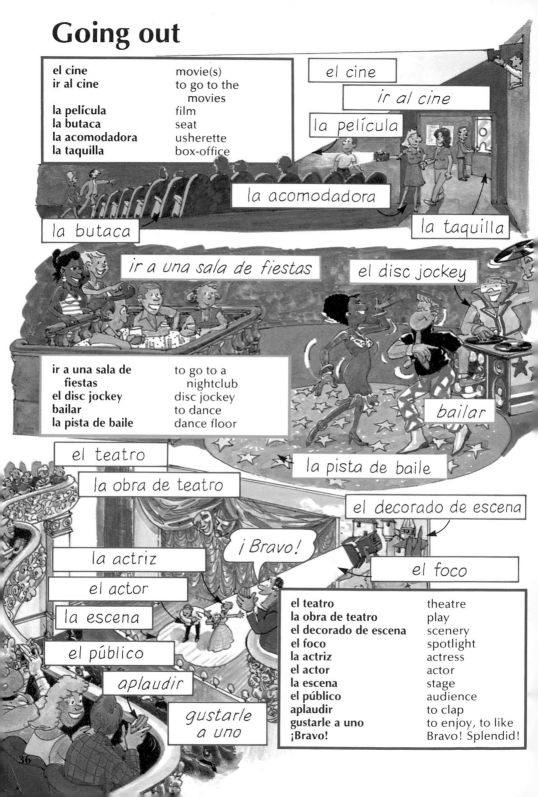

el cine	movie(s)
ir al cine	to go to the movies
la película	film
la butaca	seat
la acomodadora	usherette
la taquilla	box-office

el cine

ir al cine

la película

la acomodadora

la butaca

la taquilla

ir a una sala de fiestas

el disc jockey

ir a una sala de fiestas	to go to a nightclub
el disc jockey	disc jockey
bailar	to dance
la pista de baile	dance floor

bailar

el teatro

la obra de teatro

el decorado de escena

¡Bravo!

la actriz

el foco

el actor

la escena

el público

la pista de baile

aplaudir

gustarle a uno

el teatro	theatre
la obra de teatro	play
el decorado de escena	scenery
el foco	spotlight
la actriz	actress
el actor	actor
la escena	stage
el público	audience
aplaudir	to clap
gustarle a uno	to enjoy, to like
¡Bravo!	Bravo! Splendid!

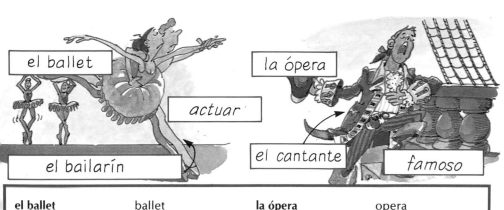

el ballet

la ópera

actuar

el cantante

el bailarín

famoso

el ballet	ballet	**la ópera**	opera
el bailarín	ballet dancer (m)	**el cantante**	singer (m)
actuar	to perform	**famoso(a)**	famous

el restorán

el camarero

El servicio no está incluido.

el menú

la cuenta

¿ Está incluido el servicio?

¿Qué van a tomar?

pedir

servir

la propina

la bandeja

para empezar

el primer plato

el postre

el restorán	restaurant	**el postre**	dessert, pudding
el camarero	waiter	**la cuenta**	bill
el menú	menu	**¿Está incluido el servicio?**	Is service included?
¿Qué van a tomar?	What would you like?	**El servicio no está incluido.**	Service is not included.
pedir	to order	**la propina**	tip
servir	to serve	**la bandeja**	tray
para empezar*	starter		
el primer plato	main course		

***Para empezar** literally means "to start with".

At the zoo

el zoológico	zoo
el animal	animal
la cebra	zebra
la jirafa	giraffe
el oso blanco	polar bear
el elefante	elephant
la trompa	trunk
el colmillo	tusk
el gorila	gorilla
salvaje	wild
manso(a)	tame
dar de comer	to feed
el guardián	keeper

el zoológico

el animal

la cebra

la jirafa

el oso blanco

el elefante

la trompa

el gorila

salvaje

manso

el colmillo

dar de comer

el guardián

In the park

el parque	park
el estanque	pond
la barca de remo	rowing boat
remar	to row
el remo	oar
la merienda	picnic
el banco	bench
descansar	to rest

el parque

el estanque

la barca de remo

remar

el remo

descansar

la merienda

el banco

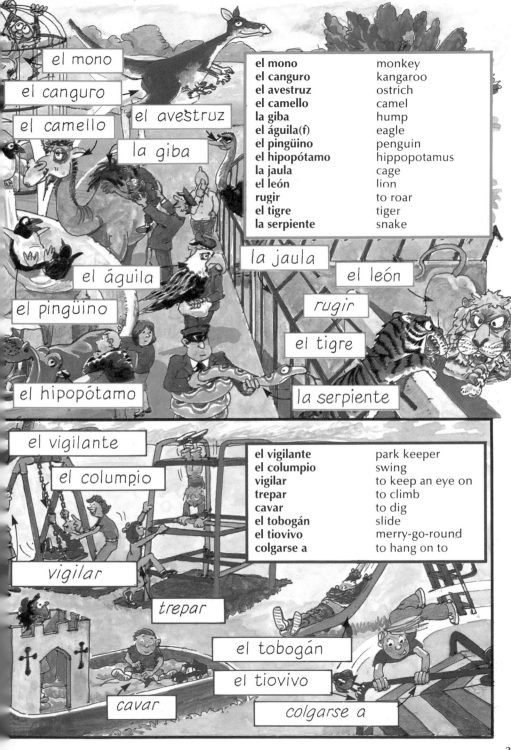

el mono

el canguro

el camello

el avestruz

la giba

el mono	monkey
el canguro	kangaroo
el avestruz	ostrich
el camello	camel
la giba	hump
el águila(f)	eagle
el pingüino	penguin
el hipopótamo	hippopotamus
la jaula	cage
el león	lion
rugir	to roar
el tigre	tiger
la serpiente	snake

la jaula

el león

el águila

rugir

el pingüino

el tigre

el hipopótamo

la serpiente

el vigilante

el columpio

el vigilante	park keeper
el columpio	swing
vigilar	to keep an eye on
trepar	to climb
cavar	to dig
el tobogán	slide
el tiovivo	merry-go-round
colgarse a	to hang on to

vigilar

trepar

el tobogán

el tiovivo

cavar

colgarse a

In the city

la ciudad

la capital

las afueras

el puente

el rascacielos

el río

la catedral

el distrito

el edificio

la iglesia

el cementerio

la capital	large town, city (also capital city)
las afueras	suburb
la ciudad	town
el rascacielos	skyscraper
la catedral	cathedral
el río	river
el puente	bridge
el distrito	district
el edificio	building
la iglesia	church
el cementerio	cemetery

el parque de bomberos

el ayuntamiento

la comisaría

el bloque de oficinas

el coche de bomberos

el coche de policia

la fábrica

la biblioteca

el parque de bomberos	fire station	el bloque de oficinas	office block
el coche de bomberos	fire engine	la comisaría	police station
la fábrica	factory	el coche de policia	police car
el ayuntamiento	town hall	la biblioteca	library

el centro	town square
la calle	street
estrecho(a)	narrow
ancho(a)	broad
la esquina	corner
atravesar la calle	to cross the street
el cruce de peatones	pedestrian crossing
el peatón	pedestrian
la plaza	square
la estatua	statue
el poste de la luz	street light
el mercado abierto	street market
el cruce subterráneo	subway

el centro

la calle

ancha

estrecha

la esquina

atravesar la caile

el cruce de peatones

el peatón

la plaza

la estatua

el mercado abierto

el poste de la luz

el cruce subterráneo

el quiosco de periódicos	newspaper stand
la paloma	pigeon
el grupo de gente	crowd
yendo y viniendo	bustling
la papelera de calle	trash can
la acera	pavement
darse prisa	to hurry
el anuncio	advertisement

el quiosco de periódicos

la paloma

el grupo de gente

yendo y viniendo

la papelera de calle

el anuncio

la acera

darse prisa

41

Shopping

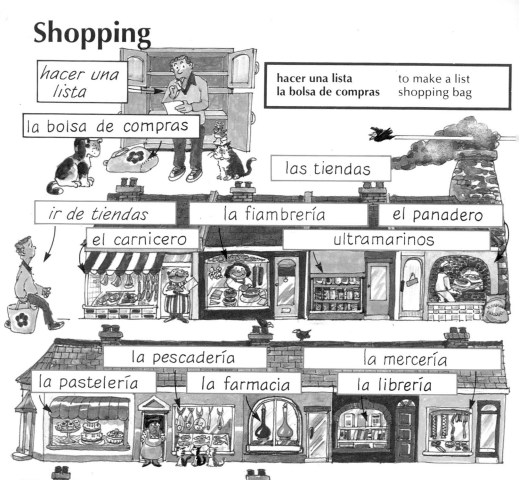

hacer una lista

la bolsa de compras

| hacer una lista | to make a list |
| la bolsa de compras | shopping bag |

las tiendas

ir de tiendas

la fiambrería

el panadero

el carnicero

ultramarinos

la pescadería

la mercería

la pastelería

la farmacia

la librería

la floristería

la tienda de discos

la peluquería

la tienda de modas

las tiendas	shops	la farmacia	pharmacy
ir de tiendas	to go shopping	la librería	bookshop
el carnicero	butcher	la mercería	needlecraft shop
la fiambrería	delicatessen	la floristería	florist
ultramarinos	grocery shop	la peluquería	hairdresser
el panadero	bakery	la tienda de discos	record shop
la pastelería	cake shop	la tienda de modas	boutique
la pescadería	fish market		

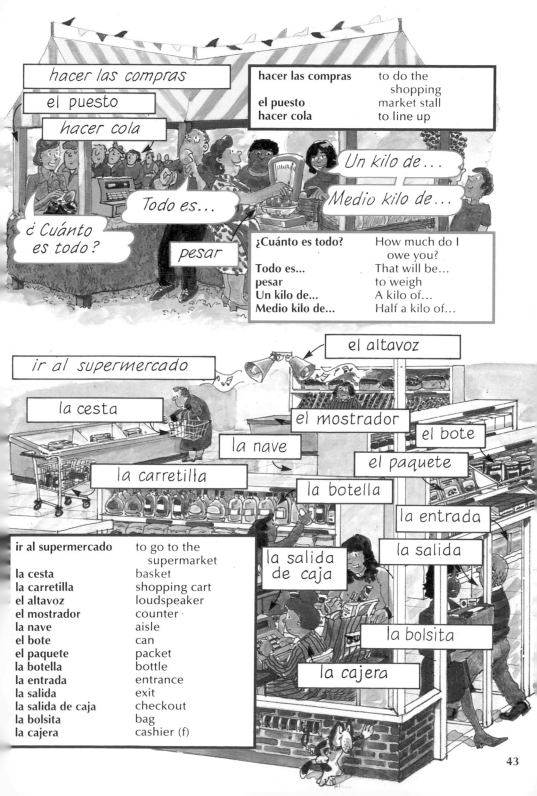

hacer las compras

el puesto

hacer cola

hacer las compras	to do the shopping
el puesto	market stall
hacer cola	to line up

Todo es...

¿Cuánto es todo?

Un kilo de...

Medio kilo de...

pesar

¿Cuánto es todo?	How much do I owe you?
Todo es...	That will be...
pesar	to weigh
Un kilo de...	A kilo of...
Medio kilo de...	Half a kilo of...

el altavoz

ir al supermercado

la cesta

el mostrador

el bote

la nave

el paquete

la carretilla

la botella

la entrada

la salida

la salida de caja

la bolsita

la cajera

ir al supermercado	to go to the supermarket
la cesta	basket
la carretilla	shopping cart
el altavoz	loudspeaker
el mostrador	counter
la nave	aisle
el bote	can
el paquete	packet
la botella	bottle
la entrada	entrance
la salida	exit
la salida de caja	checkout
la bolsita	bag
la cajera	cashier (f)

43

Shopping

ir de escaparates	to go window-shopping	**una ganga(f)**	a bargain
el escaparate	shop window	**la clienta**	customer (f)
No es caro.	It's good value.	**comprar**	to buy
Es algo caro.	It's expensive.	**la dependienta**	shop assistant (f)
SALDOS(m.pl)	SALE	**vender**	to sell

gastar dinero	to spend money	**pequeño**	small
el precio	price	**mediano**	medium
el recibo	receipt	**grande**	large
¿Qué desea?	Can I help you?	**¿Cuánto cuesta...?**	How much is...?
Querriá...	I'd like...	**Cuesta...**	It costs...
¿Qué tamaño es esto?	What size is this?		

la librería y la papelería	bookshop and stationer's	la tarjeta postal	postcard
el libro	book	el bolígrafo	ball-point pen
la edicíon de bolsillo	paperback	el lápiz	pencil
el sobre	envelope	el papel de cartas	writing paper

la librería y la papelería

el sobre

la tarjeta postal

el bolígrafo

el libro

el lápiz

la edicíon de bolsillo

el papel de cartas

los grandes almacenes

el departamento

el ascensor

la escalera móvil

juguetes

equipo de deporte

muebles

ropa

los grandes almacenes	department store	juguetes(m.pl)	toys
el departamento	department	muebles(m.pl)	furniture
la escalera móvil	escalator	equipo de deporte(m)	sports equipment
el ascensor	elevator	ropa(f)	clothing, clothes

At the post office and bank

correos(m.pl)	post office	**el telegrama**	telegram
el buzón	mailbox	**el formulario**	form
echar al correo	to mail	**el sello**	stamp
la carta	letter	**por avión**	airmail
el paquete	package	**las señas**	address
las horas de recogida	collection times	**el distrito postal**	zip code
mandar	to send		

correos

el buzón

echar al correo

la carta

las horas de recogida

mandar

el telegrama

el formulario

el paquete

por avión

el sello

las señas

el distrito postal

el cartero

el correo

entregar

el cartero	postman
el correo	mail
entregar	to deliver

el banco

el dinero

el cajero

cambiar dinero

¿Tiene cambio?

el tipo de cambio

la moneda

el gerente del banco

el billete

la tarjeta de crédito

meter dinero en el banco

sacar dinero del banco

la cartera

la chequera

hacer un cheque

el monedero

el bolso

el banco	bank	la tarjeta de crédito	credit card
el dinero	money	meter dinero en el banco	to put money in the bank
cambiar dinero	to change money	sacar dinero del banco	to take money out
el tipo de cambio	exchange rate		
el gerente del banco	bank manager		
el cajero	cashier (m)	la chequera	check-book
¿Tiene cambio?	Have you any change?	hacer un cheque	to write a check
		la cartera	wallet
la moneda	coin	el monedero	purse
el billete	paper money	el bolso	handbag

Phonecalls and letters

hacer una llamada	to make a telephone call	**la guía de teléfonos**	telephone directory
el teléfono	telephone	**sonar**	to ring
el auricular	receiver	**contestar al teléfono**	to answer the telephone
descolgar	to pick up the receiver	**¡Dígame!**	Hello!
marcar el número	to dial the number	**¿Quién habla?**	Who's speaking?
el número de teléfono	telephone number	**Soy Juanita.**	It's Juanita.
la cifra regional	area code	**Te llamo más tarde.**	I'll call you back.
		¡Adiós!	Goodbye.
		colgar	to hang up

la cabina de teléfono	telephone box
la urgencia	emergency
la llamada de urgencia	911 call

escribir una carta

el 12 de marzo de 1988

Muy señor mío:/ Estimada señora:

Gracias por su carta del...

Adjunto...

...a vuelta de correo.

Le saluda atentamente,

escribir una carta	to write a letter	**Adjunto...**	I enclose...
Muy señor mío:/ Estimada señora:	Dear Sir/Madam,	**a vuelta de correo**	by return mail
Gracias por su carta del...	Thank you for your letter of...	**Le saluda atentamente,**	Yours faithfully,

abrir una carta

el 9 de enero de 1999

Querida Juanita:

Me encantó tener noticias tuyas.

Te mando por separado...

Un abrazo de...

abrir una carta	to open a letter	**Te mando por separado...**	I am sending... separately.
Querida Juanita:	Dear Juanita,	**Un abrazo de...**	Love from...
Me encantó tener noticias tuyas.	It was lovely to hear from you.		

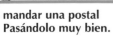

mandar una postal

mandar un telegrama

Pasándolo muy bien.

Deseando verte pronto.

Recado urgente
stop telefonea
a casa

mandar una postal	to send a postcard	**mandar un telegrama**	to send a telegram
Pasándolo muy bien.	Having a lovely time.	**Recado urgente stop telefonea a casa**	Urgent message stop telephone home
Deseando verte pronto.	Look forward to seeing you soon.		

Out and about

ir a pie	to walk	**el mapa**	map
correr	to run	**el poste indicador**	signpost
el cochecito de niños	stroller	**¿A qué distancia**	How far is...?
¿Por dónde está...?	Which way is . . . ?	**está...?**	
preguntar el camino	to ask the way		

coger el bus	to take the bus	**el bus**	bus
el pasajero	passenger (m)	**la parada de autobuses**	bus stop
bajarse	to get off	**la estación de metro**	subway
subirse	to get on		station
el billete	ticket	**el metro**	subway

el tráfico

el autocar

la furgoneta

el camión

el conductor

el auto

conducir

el ciclomotor

la bicicleta

ir en bicicleta

lenta

la motocicleta

rápida

el embotellamiento

el tráfico	traffic	**el ciclomotor**	moped
el camión	truck	**ir en bicicleta**	to ride a bicycle
la furgoneta	van	**la bicicleta**	bicycle
el autocar	tour bus	**lento(a)**	slow
el conductor	driver (m)	**la motocicleta**	motorbike
conducir	to drive	**rápido(a)**	fast
el auto	car	**el embotellamiento**	traffic jam

la parada de taxis

el taxi

parar un taxi

el precio del viaje

la parada de taxis	taxi stand
el taxi	taxi
parar un taxi	to hail a taxi
el precio del viaje	fare

Driving

arrancar

adelantar

la autopista

las luces de tráfico

la carretera

reducir velocidad

acelerar

torcer a la izquierda

torcer a la derecha

seguir todo derecho

arrancar	to start off
acelerar	to gather speed
adelantar	to pass
reducir velocidad	to slow down
la autopista	motorway
las luces de tráfico	traffic lights
la carretera	main road
torcer a la izquierda	to turn left
torcer a la derecha	to turn right
seguir todo derecho	to go straight on
la bocacalle	side street
dirección única	one way
dirección prohibida	no entry

la bocacalle

dirección única

dirección prohibida

el aparcamiento

hacia atrás

aparcar

¡Prohibido el estacionamiento!

hacia adelante

¡Prohibido el estacionamiento!	No parking!	**aparcar**	to park
		hacia atrás	backwards
el aparcamiento	car-park	**hacia adelante**	forwards

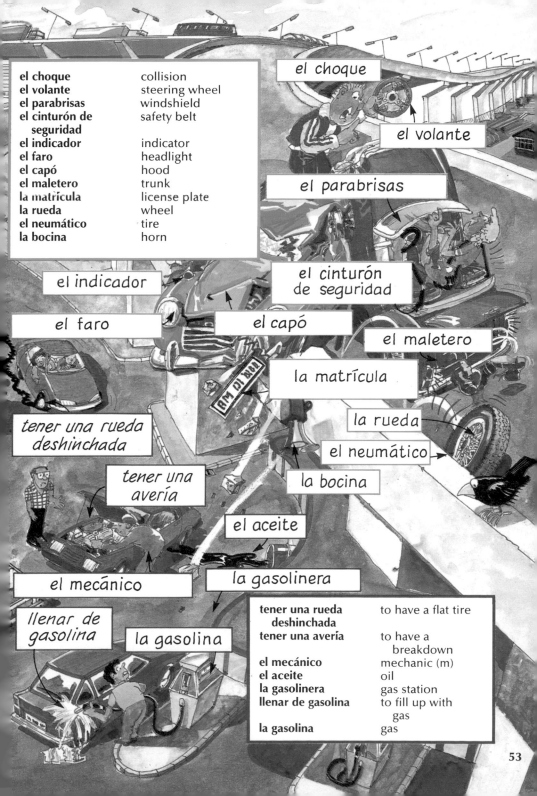

el choque	collision
el volante	steering wheel
el parabrisas	windshield
el cinturón de seguridad	safety belt
el indicador	indicator
el faro	headlight
el capó	hood
el maletero	trunk
la matrícula	license plate
la rueda	wheel
el neumático	tire
la bocina	horn

el choque

el volante

el parabrisas

el cinturón de seguridad

el indicador

el faro

el capó

el maletero

la matrícula

la rueda

el neumático

tener una rueda deshinchada

tener una avería

la bocina

el aceite

el mecánico

la gasolinera

llenar de gasolina

la gasolina

tener una rueda deshinchada	to have a flat tire
tener una avería	to have a breakdown
el mecánico	mechanic (m)
el aceite	oil
la gasolinera	gas station
llenar de gasolina	to fill up with gas
la gasolina	gas

Travelling by train

la estación

la consigna

el mozo

el revisor

la sala de espera

la barrera

el viajero

el horario

El tren para...

la taquilla

El tren desde...

el billete

el billete de ida y vuelta

el billete de abono

la máquina de billetes

reservar un asiento

el billete de andén

la estación	station	**El tren desde...**	The train from...
el mozo	porter	**la taquilla**	ticket office
la consigna	left luggage office	**el billete**	ticket
el revisor	ticket collector	**el billete de ida y**	return ticket
la sala de espera	waiting-room	**vuelta**	
la barrera	barrier	**el billete de abono**	season ticket
el viajero	traveller (m)	**la máquina de billetes**	ticket machine
el horario	timetable	**el billete de andén**	platform ticket
El tren para...	The train to...	**reservar un asiento**	to reserve a seat

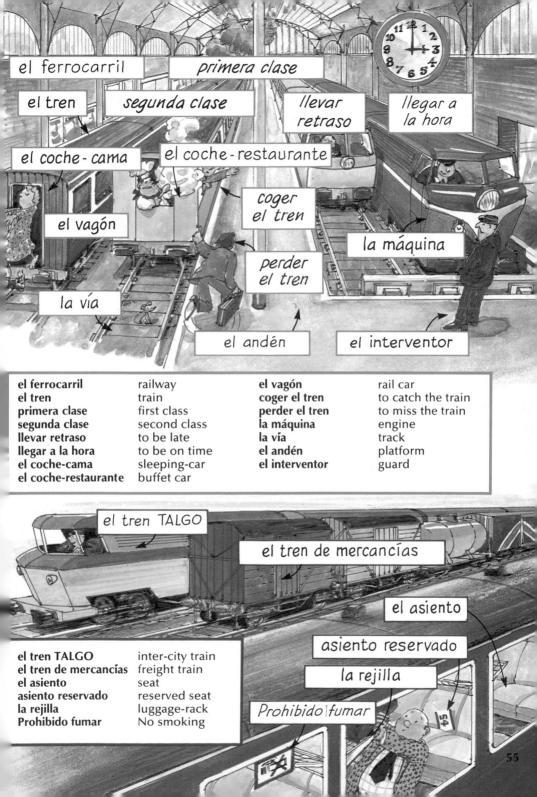

el ferrocarril

el tren

primera clase

segunda clase

llevar retraso

llegar a la hora

el coche-cama

el coche-restaurante

coger el tren

el vagón

la máquina

perder el tren

la vía

el andén

el interventor

el ferrocarril	railway	**el vagón**	rail car
el tren	train	**coger el tren**	to catch the train
primera clase	first class	**perder el tren**	to miss the train
segunda clase	second class	**la máquina**	engine
llevar retraso	to be late	**la vía**	track
llegar a la hora	to be on time	**el andén**	platform
el coche-cama	sleeping-car	**el interventor**	guard
el coche-restaurante	buffet car		

el tren TALGO

el tren de mercancías

el asiento

asiento reservado

la rejilla

Prohibido fumar

el tren TALGO	inter-city train
el tren de mercancías	freight train
el asiento	seat
asiento reservado	reserved seat
la rejilla	luggage-rack
Prohibido fumar	No smoking

55

Travelling by plane and boat

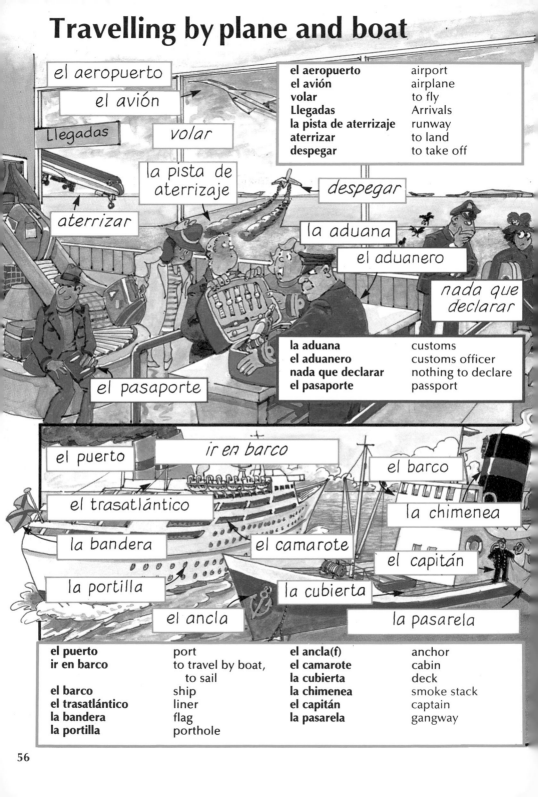

el aeropuerto

el avión

Llegadas

volar

la pista de aterrizaje

aterrizar

despegar

la aduana

el aduanero

nada que declarar

el pasaporte

el aeropuerto	airport
el avión	airplane
volar	to fly
Llegadas	Arrivals
la pista de aterrizaje	runway
aterrizar	to land
despegar	to take off

la aduana	customs
el aduanero	customs officer
nada que declarar	nothing to declare
el pasaporte	passport

el puerto

ir en barco

el barco

el trasatlántico

la chimenea

la bandera

el camarote

el capitán

la portilla

la cubierta

el ancla

la pasarela

el puerto	port	**el ancla(f)**	anchor
ir en barco	to travel by boat, to sail	**el camarote**	cabin
		la cubierta	deck
el barco	ship	**la chimenea**	smoke stack
el trasatlántico	liner	**el capitán**	captain
la bandera	flag	**la pasarela**	gangway
la portilla	porthole		

Salidas	Departures	el piloto	pilot
la tienda libre de impuestos	duty-free shop	la tripulación	crew
la recepción	check-in	la azafata	stewardess
el billete	ticket	abordar el avión	to board the plane
la etiqueta	label	la maleta	suitcase
la carretilla	luggage cart	el equipaje de mano	hand luggage
¡Abrocharse el cinturón!	Fasten your seatbelts.		

Salidas

la tienda libre de impuestos

¡Abrocharse el cinturón!

el piloto

la tripulación

la recepción

la azafata

la maleta

abordar el avión

el billete

la etiqueta

el equipaje de mano

la carretilla

el ferry

los muelles

la travesía

marearse

la carga

cargar

descargar

la bodega

el marinero

el ferry	ferry
la travesía	crossing
marearse	to be seasick
los muelles	docks
la carga	cargo
cargar	to load
descargar	to unload
la bodega	hold
el marinero	sailor

Vacations

ir de vacaciones

la turista

hacer la maleta

ir de vacaciones	to go on vacation
hacer la maleta	to pack
el aceite para el sol	suntan oil
las gafas de sol	sunglasses
la turista	tourist (f)
visitar los lugares de interés	to sightsee

el aceite para el sol

las gafas de sol

visitar los lugares de interés

el hotel

quedarse en un hotel

la recepción

el mozo

con ducha

la habitación individual

con balcón

la habitación doble

reservar una habitación

la pensión

estar completo

el hotel	hotel	**reservar una habitación**	to reserve a room
quedarse en un hotel	to stay in a hotel	**estar completo**	to be fully booked
la recepción	reception	**con ducha**	with shower
el mozo	porter	**con balcón**	with balcony
la habitación individual	single room	**la pensión**	guest house, boarding house
la habitación doble	double room		

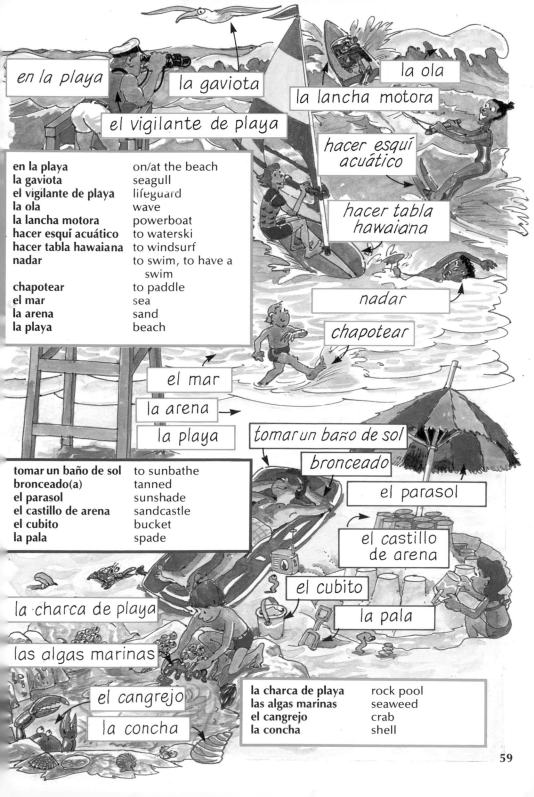

en la playa

la gaviota

el vigilante de playa

la ola

la lancha motora

hacer esquí acuático

hacer tabla hawaiana

nadar

chapotear

en la playa	on/at the beach
la gaviota	seagull
el vigilante de playa	lifeguard
la ola	wave
la lancha motora	powerboat
hacer esquí acuático	to waterski
hacer tabla hawaiana	to windsurf
nadar	to swim, to have a swim
chapotear	to paddle
el mar	sea
la arena	sand
la playa	beach

el mar

la arena

la playa

tomar un baño de sol

bronceado

el parasol

el castillo de arena

el cubito

la pala

tomar un baño de sol	to sunbathe
bronceado(a)	tanned
el parasol	sunshade
el castillo de arena	sandcastle
el cubito	bucket
la pala	spade

la charca de playa

las algas marinas

el cangrejo

la concha

la charca de playa	rock pool
las algas marinas	seaweed
el cangrejo	crab
la concha	shell

Vacations

hacer el alpinismo	to go mountaineering
la montaña	mountain
la cima	summit
la vista	view
empinado(a)	steep
escalar	to climb
el alpinista	climber (m)
la mochila	rucksack, backpack

esquiar

el centro de esquí

la silla de ascenso

hacer el alpinismo

la cima

la vista

la montaña

empinado

escalar

el alpinista

la mochila

el instructor de esquí

la pista

el tobogán

el bastón de esquí

las botas de esquí

los esquís

esquiar	to go skiing
el centro de esquí	ski resort
la silla de ascenso	chairlift
el instructor de esquí	ski instructor (m)
la pista	ski slope, ski run
el tobogán	toboggan
el bastón de esquí	ski pole
las botas de esquí	ski boots
los esquís	skis

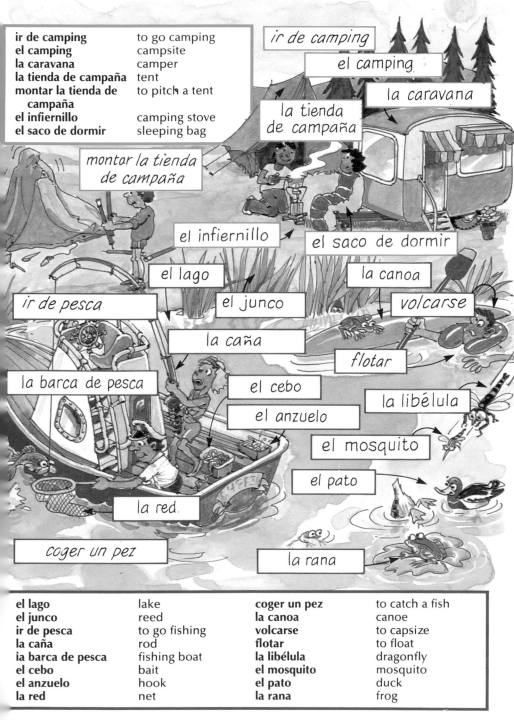

ir de camping	to go camping
el camping	campsite
la caravana	camper
la tienda de campaña	tent
montar la tienda de campaña	to pitch a tent
el infiernillo	camping stove
el saco de dormir	sleeping bag

ir de camping

el camping

la caravana

la tienda de campaña

montar la tienda de campaña

el infiernillo

el saco de dormir

el lago

la canoa

ir de pesca

el junco

volcarse

la caña

flotar

la barca de pesca

el cebo

la libélula

el anzuelo

el mosquito

el pato

la red.

coger un pez

la rana

el lago	lake	**coger un pez**	to catch a fish
el junco	reed	**la canoa**	canoe
ir de pesca	to go fishing	**volcarse**	to capsize
la caña	rod	**flotar**	to float
la barca de pesca	fishing boat	**la libélula**	dragonfly
el cebo	bait	**el mosquito**	mosquito
el anzuelo	hook	**el pato**	duck
la red	net	**la rana**	frog

In the countryside

el pueblo

el paisaje

tranquilo

el campo

la casita

dar un paseo

el camino

el prado

el arroyo

el conejo

el topo

trepar un árbol

las flores del campo

coger flores

un manojo de flores

la margarita

la amapola

el pueblo	village
el paisaje	landscape
tranquilo(a)	peaceful
el campo	countryside
la casita	cottage
dar un paseo	to go for a walk

el camino	path
el arroyo	stream
el prado	meadow
el conejo	rabbit
el topo	mole
trepar un árbol	to climb a tree
las flores del campo	wild flowers
coger flores	to pick flowers
un manojo de flores	a bunch of flowers
la margarita	daisy
la amapola	poppy

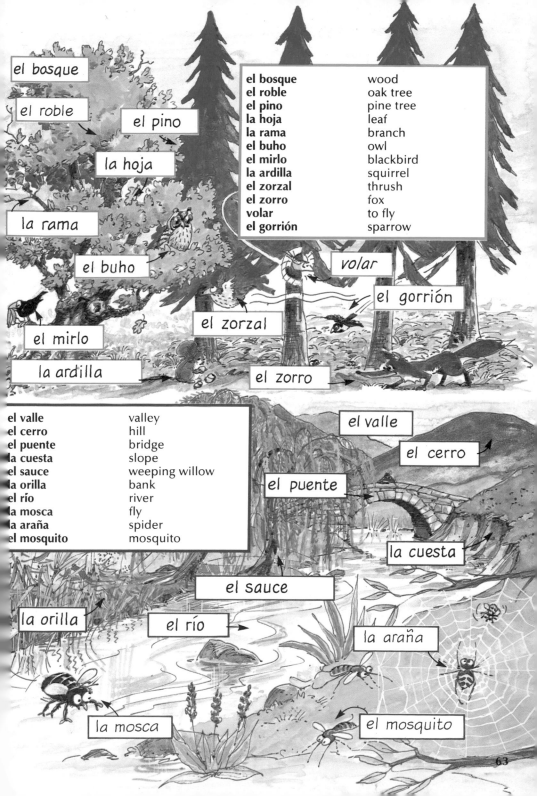

el bosque

el roble

el pino

la hoja

la rama

el buho

el mirlo

la ardilla

el zorzal

volar

el gorrión

el zorro

el bosque	wood
el roble	oak tree
el pino	pine tree
la hoja	leaf
la rama	branch
el buho	owl
el mirlo	blackbird
la ardilla	squirrel
el zorzal	thrush
el zorro	fox
volar	to fly
el gorrión	sparrow

el valle

el cerro

el puente

la cuesta

el sauce

la orilla

el río

la araña

la mosca

el mosquito

el valle	valley
el cerro	hill
el puente	bridge
la cuesta	slope
el sauce	weeping willow
la orilla	bank
el río	river
la mosca	fly
la araña	spider
el mosquito	mosquito

On the farm

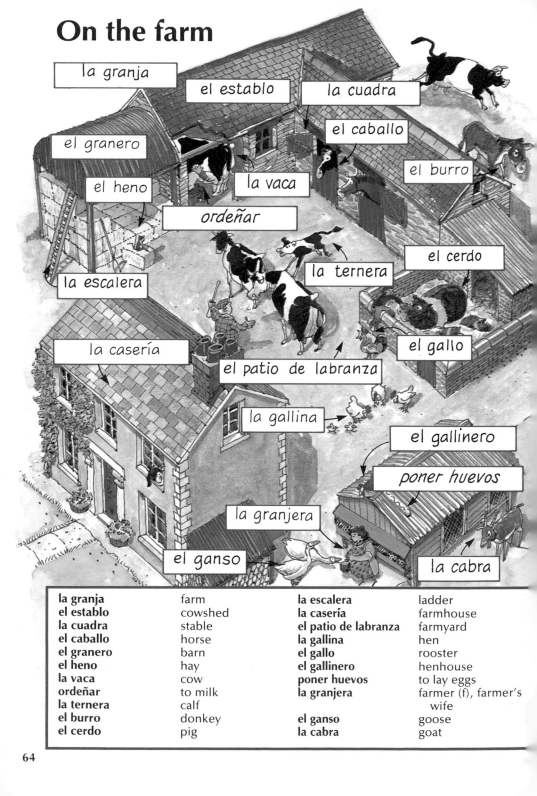

la granja

el establo

la cuadra

el caballo

el granero

el burro

el heno

la vaca

ordeñar

la escalera

el cerdo

la ternera

la casería

el gallo

el patio de labranza

la gallina

el gallinero

poner huevos

la granjera

el ganso

la cabra

la granja	farm	**la escalera**	ladder
el establo	cowshed	**la casería**	farmhouse
la cuadra	stable	**el patio de labranza**	farmyard
el caballo	horse	**la gallina**	hen
el granero	barn	**el gallo**	rooster
el heno	hay	**el gallinero**	henhouse
la vaca	cow	**poner huevos**	to lay eggs
ordeñar	to milk	**la granjera**	farmer (f), farmer's
la ternera	calf		wife
el burro	donkey	**el ganso**	goose
el cerdo	pig	**la cabra**	goat

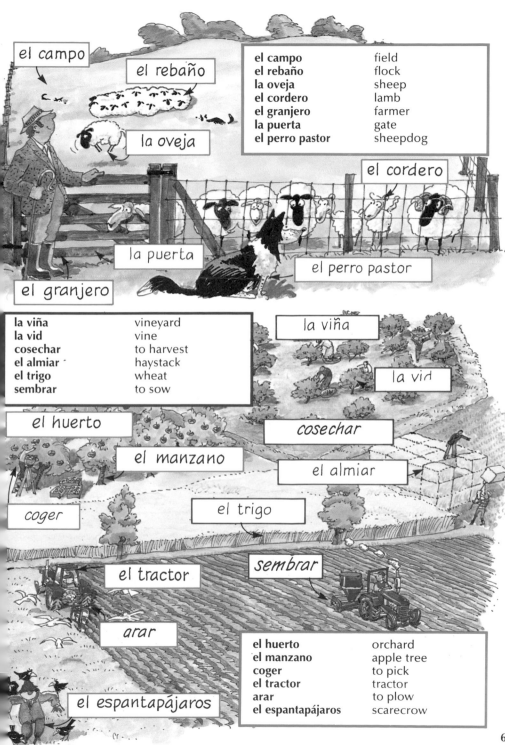

el campo

el rebaño

la oveja

el campo	field
el rebaño	flock
la oveja	sheep
el cordero	lamb
el granjero	farmer
la puerta	gate
el perro pastor	sheepdog

el cordero

la puerta

el perro pastor

el granjero

la viña	vineyard
la vid	vine
cosechar	to harvest
el almiar	haystack
el trigo	wheat
sembrar	to sow

la viña

la vid

el huerto

cosechar

el manzano

el almiar

coger

el trigo

el tractor

sembrar

arar

el espantapájaros

el huerto	orchard
el manzano	apple tree
coger	to pick
el tractor	tractor
arar	to plow
el espantapájaros	scarecrow

At work

ir a trabajar

llegar tarde

llegar a tiempo

la hora de comer

horas extraordinarias

ir a trabajar	to go to work	**la hora de comer**	lunch hour
llegar tarde	to be late	**horas extraordinarias**	overtime
llegar a tiempo	to be on time		

la oficina

emplear a alguien

trabajadoras

jubilarse

la jefa

la secretaria

el empleado

perezoso

despedir a alguien

la oficina	office	**el empleado**	employee (m)
la jefa	boss (f)	**trabajador(a)**	hard-working
la secretaria	secretary (f)	**perezoso(a)**	lazy
emplear a alguien	to employ someone	**jubilarse**	to retire
		despedir a alguien	to fire someone

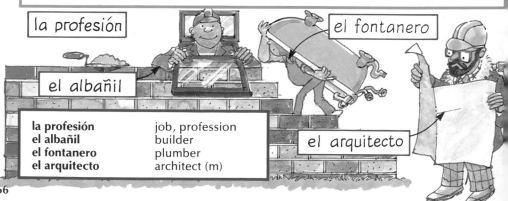

la profesión

el albañil

el fontanero

el arquitecto

la profesión	job, profession
el albañil	builder
el fontanero	plumber
el arquitecto	architect (m)

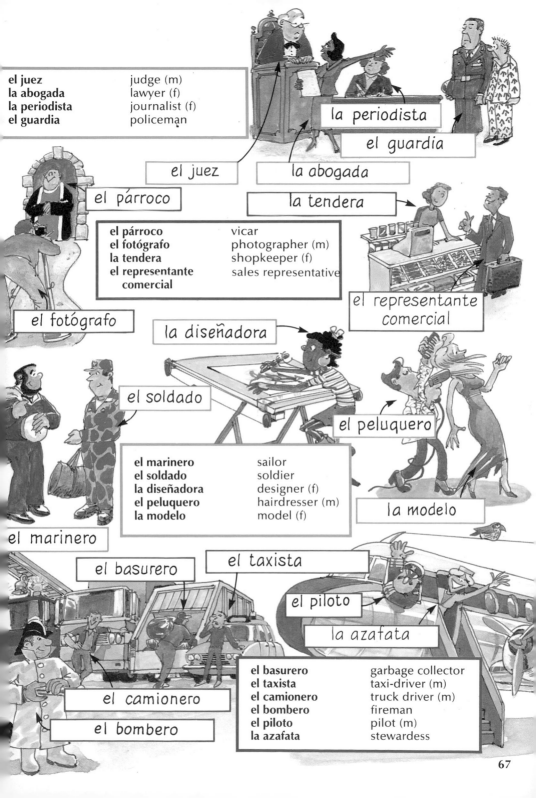

el juez	judge (m)
la abogada	lawyer (f)
la periodista	journalist (f)
el guardia	policeman

la periodista

el guardia

el juez

la abogada

el párroco

la tendera

el párroco	vicar
el fotógrafo	photographer (m)
la tendera	shopkeeper (f)
el representante comercial	sales representative

el fotógrafo

el representante comercial

la diseñadora

el soldado

el peluquero

el marinero	sailor
el soldado	soldier
la diseñadora	designer (f)
el peluquero	hairdresser (m)
la modelo	model (f)

la modelo

el marinero

el taxista

el basurero

el piloto

la azafata

el camionero

el basurero	garbage collector
el taxista	taxi-driver (m)
el camionero	truck driver (m)
el bombero	fireman
el piloto	pilot (m)
la azafata	stewardess

el bombero

Illness and health

sentirse malo

tomar la temperatura

el termómetro

tener fiebre

la médica

la receta

sentirse mejor

curar

la pastilla

sano

sentirse malo(a)	to feel ill	**la médica**	doctor (f)
tomar la temperatura	to take someone's temperature	**la receta**	prescription
el termómetro	thermometer	**curar**	to cure
tener fiebre	to have a temperature	**la pastilla**	pill
		sentirse mejor	to feel better
		sano(a)	healthy

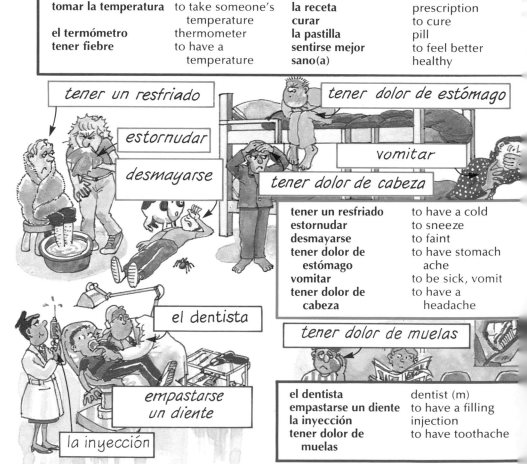

tener un resfriado

estornudar

desmayarse

tener dolor de estómago

vomitar

tener dolor de cabeza

tener un resfriado	to have a cold
estornudar	to sneeze
desmayarse	to faint
tener dolor de estómago	to have stomach ache
vomitar	to be sick, vomit
tener dolor de cabeza	to have a headache

el dentista

empastarse un diente

la inyección

tener dolor de muelas

el dentista	dentist (m)
empastarse un diente	to have a filling
la inyección	injection
tener dolor de muelas	to have toothache

el hospital

urgencias

la quemadura

dislocarse la muñeca

la contusión

romperse la pierna

la cortadura

el esparadrapo

la venda

el hospital	hospital	la quemadura	burn
urgencias	emergency room	dislocarse la muñeca	to sprain your wrist
romperse la pierna	to break your leg	el esparadrapo	adhesive bandage
la contusión	bruise	la venda	bandage
la cortadura	cut		

la ambulancia

tomar el pulso

el paciente

la camilla

la ambulancia	ambulance
tomar el pulso	to take someone's pulse
la camilla	stretcher
el paciente	patient (m)

el quirófano

la intervención cirúrgica

la enfermera

el cirujano

el quirófano	operating theatre
el cirujano	surgeon (m)
la intervención cirúrgica	operation
la enfermera	nurse (f)

School and education

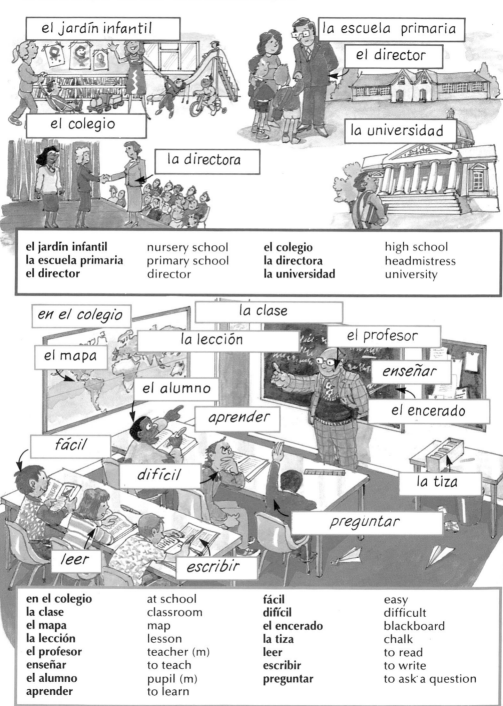

el jardín infantil

la escuela primaria

el director

el colegio

la directora

la universidad

el jardín infantil	nursery school	**el colegio**	high school
la escuela primaria	primary school	**la directora**	headmistress
el director	director	**la universidad**	university

en el colegio

la clase

la lección

el profesor

el mapa

enseñar

el alumno

el encerado

aprender

fácil

difícil

la tiza

preguntar

leer

escribir

en el colegio	at school	**fácil**	easy
la clase	classroom	**difícil**	difficult
el mapa	map	**el encerado**	blackboard
la lección	lesson	**la tiza**	chalk
el profesor	teacher (m)	**leer**	to read
enseñar	to teach	**escribir**	to write
el alumno	pupil (m)	**preguntar**	to ask a question
aprender	to learn		

la cartera	satchel
el cuaderno	exercise book
la caja de lápices	pencil case
la pluma	pen
el bolígrafo	ball-point pen
el lápiz	pencil
la goma	eraser
la regla	ruler

la cartera

el cuaderno

la caja de lápices

la pluma

el bolígrafo

la goma

la regla

el lápiz

en el jardín infantil

el juguete

en el jardín infantil	at nursery school
el juguete	toy
el lápiz de color	crayon
el libro de imágenes	picture book
jugar	to play

el lápiz de color

el libro de imágenes

jugar

el patio de juego

la campana

el guardarropa

el descanso

el patio de juego	playground
el descanso	break
la campana	bell
el guardarropa	coatroom

71

School and education

el curso

el horario

la asignatura

el español

las matemáticas

el principio
de curso

la física

el francés

la química

el inglés

la biología

el alemán

la historia

la geografía

el fin de curso

la música

la informática

la gimnasia

el curso	course, academic year	**el alemán**	German
el principio de curso	beginning of course	**las matemáticas**	math
		la física	physics
		la química	chemistry
el fin de curso	end of course	**la biología**	biology
el horario	timetable	**la historia**	history
la asignatura	subject	**la geografía**	geography
el español	Spanish	**la música**	music
el francés	French	**la informática**	computer studies
el inglés	English	**la gimnasia**	PE

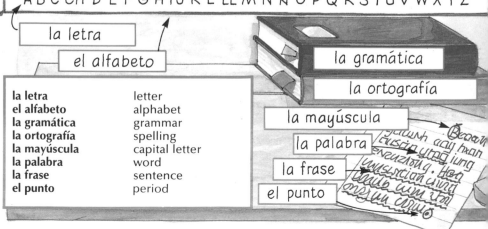

A B C CH D E F G H I J K L LL M N Ñ O P Q R S T U V W X Y Z

la letra

el alfabeto

la gramática

la ortografía

la letra	letter
el alfabeto	alphabet
la gramática	grammar
la ortografía	spelling
la mayúscula	capital letter
la palabra	word
la frase	sentence
el punto	period

la mayúscula

la palabra

la frase

el punto

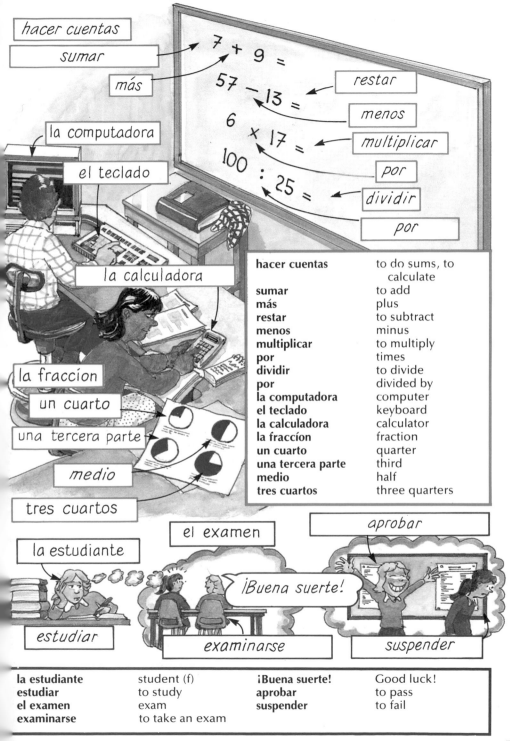

hacer cuentas

sumar

más

$7 + 9 =$

$57 - 13 =$

restar

menos

$6 \times 17 =$

multiplicar

por

$100 : 25 =$

dividir

por

la computadora

el teclado

la calculadora

la fraccíon

un cuarto

una tercera parte

medio

tres cuartos

hacer cuentas	to do sums, to calculate
sumar	to add
más	plus
restar	to subtract
menos	minus
multiplicar	to multiply
por	times
dividir	to divide
por	divided by
la computadora	computer
el teclado	keyboard
la calculadora	calculator
la fraccíon	fraction
un cuarto	quarter
una tercera parte	third
medio	half
tres cuartos	three quarters

el examen

aprobar

la estudiante

¡Buena suerte!

estudiar

examinarse

suspender

la estudiante	student (f)	¡Buena suerte!	Good luck!
estudiar	to study	aprobar	to pass
el examen	exam	suspender	to fail
examinarse	to take an exam		

Shapes and sizes

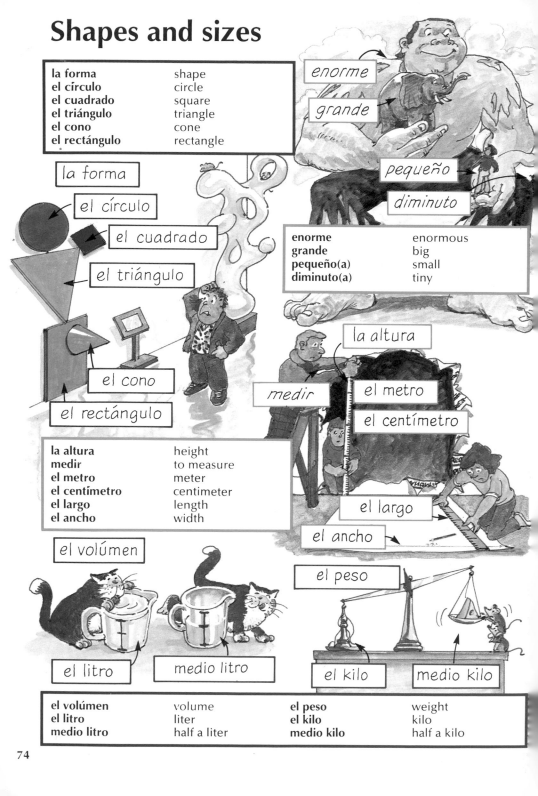

la forma	shape
el círculo	circle
el cuadrado	square
el triángulo	triangle
el cono	cone
el rectángulo	rectangle

la forma

el círculo

el cuadrado

el triángulo

el cono

el rectángulo

enorme

grande

pequeño

diminuto

enorme	enormous
grande	big
pequeño(a)	small
diminuto(a)	tiny

la altura

medir

el metro

el centímetro

el largo

el ancho

la altura	height
medir	to measure
el metro	meter
el centímetro	centimeter
el largo	length
el ancho	width

el volúmen

el peso

el litro

medio litro

el kilo

medio kilo

el volúmen	volume		**el peso**	weight
el litro	liter		**el kilo**	kilo
medio litro	half a liter		**medio kilo**	half a kilo

Numbers

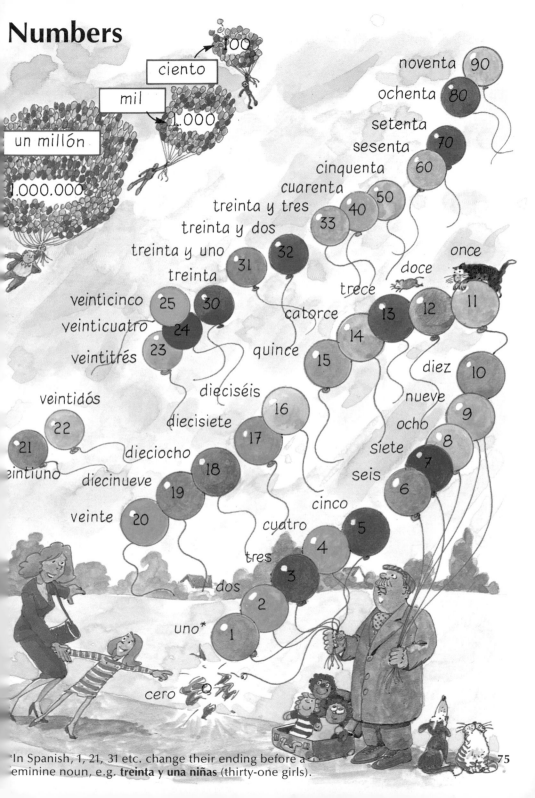

ciento — 100

mil → 1.000

un millón — 1.000.000

noventa — 90
ochenta — 80
setenta
sesenta — 70
cinquenta — 60
cuarenta — 50
treinta y tres — 40
treinta y dos — 33
treinta y uno — 32
treinta — 31
veinticinco — 30
veinticuatro — 25
veintitrés — 24
— 23
veintidós — 22
— 21
veintiuno
veinte — 20
diecinueve — 19
dieciocho — 18
diecisiete — 17
dieciséis — 16
quince — 15
catorce — 14
trece — 13
doce — 12
once — 11
diez — 10
nueve — 9
ocho — 8
siete — 7
seis — 6
cinco — 5
cuatro — 4
tres — 3
dos — 2
uno* — 1
cero — 0

*In Spanish, 1, 21, 31 etc. change their ending before a feminine noun, e.g. **treinta y una niñas** (thirty-one girls).

Sport

mantenerse en forma

hacer fúting

la sudadera

entrenarse

los zapatos de corredor

el traje de entrenamiento

mantenerse en forma	to keep fit	**los zapatos de corredor**	running shoes
entrenarse	to exercise	**el traje de entrenamiento**	tracksuit
hacer fúting	to jog		
la sudadera	headband		

jugar al golf

el palo de golf

jugar al tenis

la pista de tenis

el tenista

Dentro

servir

Fuera

jugar al scuach

la red

la pelota

la raqueta

jugar al tenis	to play tennis	**la red**	net
la pista de tenis	tennis court	**la pelota**	ball
el tenista	tennis player (m)	**la raqueta**	racket
servir	to serve	**jugar al golf**	to play golf
Dentro	In	**el palo de golf**	golf club
Fuera	Out	**jugar al scuach**	to play squash

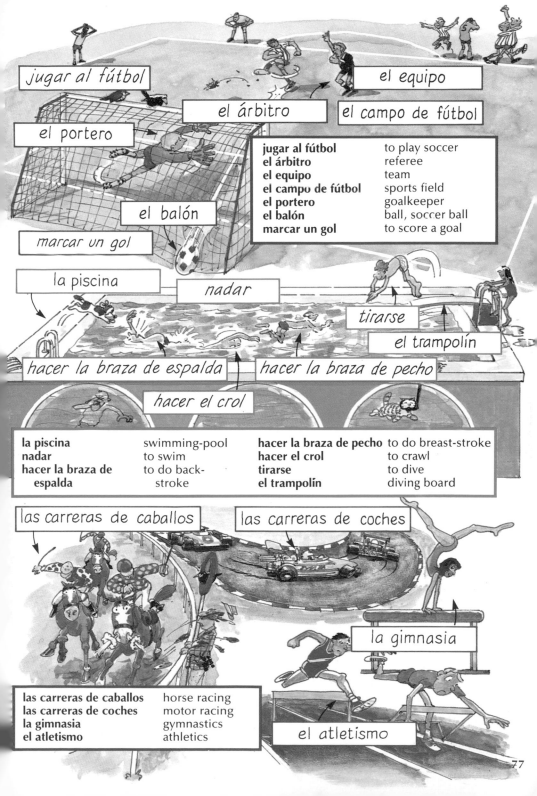

jugar al fútbol

el equipo

el árbitro

el campo de fútbol

el portero

el balón

marcar un gol

jugar al fútbol	to play soccer
el árbitro	referee
el equipo	team
el campo de fútbol	sports field
el portero	goalkeeper
el balón	ball, soccer ball
marcar un gol	to score a goal

la piscina

nadar

tirarse

el trampolín

hacer la braza de espalda

hacer la braza de pecho

hacer el crol

la piscina	swimming-pool	**hacer la braza de pecho**	to do breast-stroke
nadar	to swim	**hacer el crol**	to crawl
hacer la braza de espalda	to do back-stroke	**tirarse**	to dive
		el trampolín	diving board

las carreras de caballos

las carreras de coches

la gimnasia

el atletismo

las carreras de caballos	horse racing
las carreras de coches	motor racing
la gimnasia	gymnastics
el atletismo	athletics

77

Celebrations

el cumpleaños	birthday
la fiesta	party
el globo	balloon
¡Felicidades!	Congratulations!
invitar	to invite
divertirse	to have fun, to enjoy yourself
la tarta	cake
la vela	candle
la tarjeta	card
el regalo	present
la envoltura	wrapping

el cumpleaños

la fiesta

el globo

¡Felicidades!

invitar

divertirse

la tarta

la vela

la tarjeta

el regalo

la envoltura

el Día de Navidad

Pascua

las Navidades

los Reyes Magos

el árbol de Navidad

Pascua	Easter
las Navidades	Christmas
el Día de Navidad	Christmas Day
los Reyes Magos	the Three Wise Men
el árbol de Navidad	Christmas tree

hacerse novios	to get engaged
la boda	wedding
casarse	to get married
el novio	bridegroom
la novia	bride
el invitado	guest (m)
felicitar	to congratulate
el ramo de flores	bouquet
ser feliz	to be happy
el viaje de novios	honeymoon

¡Felices Pascuas!*	Merry Christmas.
el villancico	carol
regalar	to give (a present)
recibir	to receive
¡Muchas gracias!	Thank you.
dar las gracias	to thank

Nochevieja	New Year's Eve
el día de Año Nuevo	New Year's Day
celebrar	to celebrate
¡Feliz Año!	Happy New Year.

*In the singular, **Pascua** means "Easter", but here **"Pascuas"** (plural) means "Christmas".

Days and dates

el calendario

el mes

enero
febrero
marzo
abril
mayo
junio
julio
agosto
setiembre
octubre
noviembre
diciembre

el año

lunes
martes
miércoles
jueves
viernes
sábado
domingo

el día

la semana

el fin de semana

el calendario	calendar
el mes	month
enero	January
febrero	February
marzo	March
abril	April
mayo	May
junio	June
julio	July
agosto	August
setiembre	September
octubre	October
noviembre	November
diciembre	December
el año	year
el día	day
la semana	week
el fin de semana	week-end
lunes (m)	Monday
martes (m)	Tuesday
miércoles (m)	Wednesday
jueves (m)	Thursday
viernes (m)	Friday
sábado (m)	Saturday
domingo (m)	Sunday

la agenda	diary
la fecha	date
martes, dos* de junio…	on Tuesday, the 2nd of June…
el primero	the first
el dos	the second
el tres	the third
el cuatro	the fourth
el cinco	the fifth

la agenda

la fecha

martes, dos de junio

el primero

el dos

el tres

el cuatro

el cinco

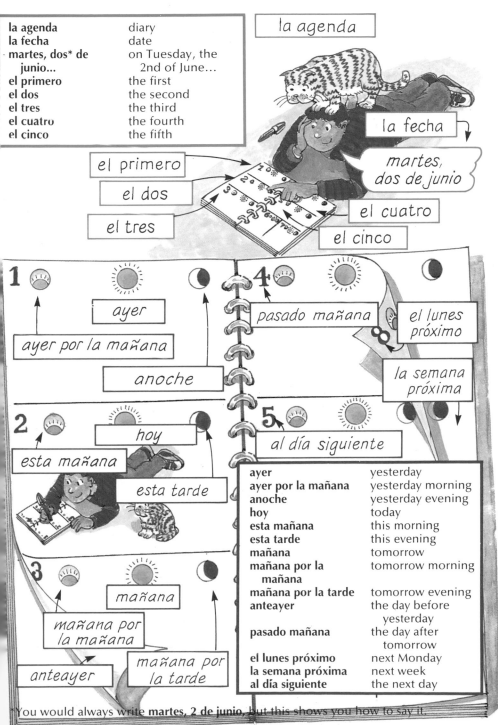

1 ayer

ayer por la mañana

anoche

2 hoy

esta mañana

esta tarde

3 mañana

mañana por la mañana

mañana por la tarde

anteayer

4 pasado mañana

el lunes próximo

la semana próxima

5 al día siguiente

ayer	yesterday
ayer por la mañana	yesterday morning
anoche	yesterday evening
hoy	today
esta mañana	this morning
esta tarde	this evening
mañana	tomorrow
mañana por la mañana	tomorrow morning
mañana por la tarde	tomorrow evening
anteayer	the day before yesterday
pasado mañana	the day after tomorrow
el lunes próximo	next Monday
la semana próxima	next week
al día siguiente	the next day

*You would always write **martes, 2 de junio**, but this shows you how to say it.

Time

el amanecer	dawn	**el sol**	sun
la salida del sol	sunrise	**el cielo**	sky
Amanece.	It is getting light.	**Es de día.**	It is light.
la mañana	morning	**el día**	day, daytime

la tarde	afternoon, evening	**las estrellas**	stars
la puesta del sol	sunset	**la luna**	moon
Oscurece.	It is getting dark.	**Es de noche.**	It is dark.
la noche	night		

¿Qué hora es?	What time is it?	**las diez menos cuarto**	a quarter to 10
la hora	hour	**las diez y cinco**	five past 10
el minuto	minute	**las diez y cuarto**	a quarter past 10
el segundo	second	**las diez y media**	half past 10
Es la una.	It is 1 o'clock.	**las ocho de la mañana**	8 a.m.
Son las tres.	It is 3 o'clock.		
mediodía	midday	**las ocho de la noche**	8 p.m.
medianoche	midnight		

el tiempo

el futuro

el pasado

el presente

en el futuro

entonces

ahora

el tiempo	time	**entonces**	then
el pasado	past	**en el futuro**	in the future
el futuro	future	**ahora**	now
el presente	present		

Weather and seasons

la estación	season
la primavera	spring
el verano	summer
el otoño	autumn
el invierno	winter

la estación

la primavera

el tiempo

Llueve.

el invierno

la lluvia

la tormenta

la nube

el otoño

el verano

los relámpagos

los truenos

el arcoiris

el paraguas

las botas de goma

estar calado

el charco

la gota de lluvia

el granizo

la inundación

el tiempo	weather
Llueve.	It's raining.
la lluvia	rain
la tormenta	storm
la nube	cloud
los relámpagos	lightning
los truenos	thunder
el paraguas	umbrella
el arcoiris	rainbow
las botas de goma	rubber boots
estar calado(a)	to be soaked to the skin
el charco	puddle
la gota de lluvia	raindrop
el granizo	hail
la inundación	flood

el clima	climate
el pronóstico del tiempo	weather forecast
¿Qué tiempo hace?	What is the weather like?

Hace bueno.	It's fine.
Brilla el sol.	The sun is shining.
sudar	to sweat
Tengo calor.	I'm hot.

el viento	wind
Hace viento.	It's windy.
la niebla	fog
Hay niebla.	It's foggy.

Hace frío.	It's cold.
estar helado(a)	to be frozen
la escarcha	frost
el carámbano	icicle
la nieve	snow
el hombre de nieve	snowman
Nieva.	It's snowing.
deshelar	to thaw

World and universe

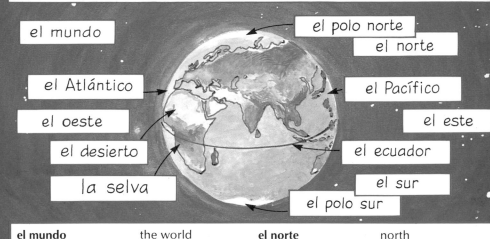

el mundo

el polo norte

el norte

el Atlántico

el Pacífico

el oeste

el este

el desierto

el ecuador

la selva

el sur

el polo sur

el mundo	the world	**el norte**	north
el Atlántico	Atlantic Ocean	**el Pacífico**	Pacific Ocean
el oeste	west	**el este**	east
el desierto	desert	**el ecuador**	Equator
la selva	jungle	**el sur**	south
el polo norte	North Pole	**el polo sur**	South Pole

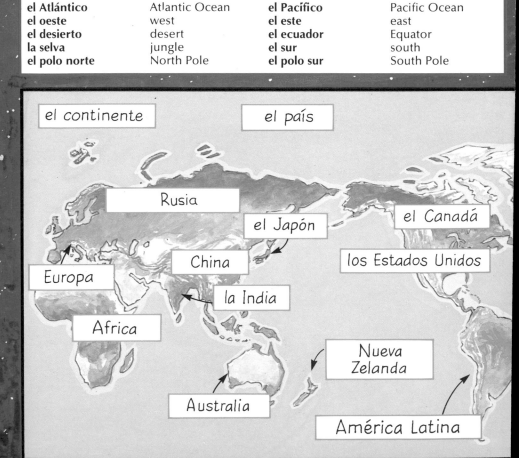

el continente

el país

Rusia

el Japón

el Canadá

China

los Estados Unidos

Europa

la India

Africa

Nueva
Zelanda

Australia

América Latina

el universo

el espacio

la estrella

el planeta

la nave espacial

la galaxia

el telescopio

el universo	universe
el espacio	space
el planeta	planet
la estrella	star
la nave espacial	spaceship
la galaxia	galaxy
el telescopio	telescope

el continente	continent
el país	country
Rusia	Russia
Europa	Europe
Africa	Africa
el Japón	Japan
China	China
la India	India
Australia	Australia
Nueva Zelanda	New Zealand
el Canadá	Canada
los Estados Unidos	United States
América Latina	Latin America

Escandinavia	Scandinavia
Gran Bretaña	Great Britain
Holanda	Netherlands
Bélgica	Belgium
Alemania	Germany
Francia	France
Suiza	Switzerland
Italia	Italy
España	Spain
Austria	Austria

Escandinavia

Gran Bretaña

Bélgica / Holanda

Francia

Alemania

Suiza

Austria

Italia

España

Politics

el presidente

el parlamento

la diputada

el primer ministro

el gobierno

el presidente	president (m)
el parlamento	parliament
la diputada	member of parliament (f)
el primer ministro	prime minister (m)
el gobierno	government

el partido

la jefa

popular

el miembro

el partido	party
la jefa	leader (f)
popular	popular
el miembro	member (m/f)

la elección

votar

de izquierdas

de centro

de derechas

ganar

perder

asociarse

pertenecer a

la elección	election	de centro	liberal
votar	to vote	de derechas	right wing
ganar	to win	asociarse	to join
perder	to lose	pertenecer a	to belong to
de izquierdas	left wing		

los medios de comunicación	the media		
entrevistar	to interview		
importante	important		
interesante	interesting		
el periódico	newspaper		
las noticias	news		
los titulares	headlines		
el artículo	article		
verdadero(a)	true		
falso(a)	false		

los medios de comunicación

entrevistar

importante

interesante

el periódico

las noticias

los titulares

el artículo

verdadero

falso

la política

la sociedad

democrática

el salario

los impuestos

el sindicato

el paro

la política	politics	los impuestos	taxes
la sociedad	society	el sindicato	trade union
democrático(a)	democratic	el paro	unemployment
el salario	salary, wages		

Describing things

ruidoso

callado

obediente

iguales

travieso

ruidoso(a)	noisy
callado(a)	quiet
obediente	obedient
travieso(a)	naughty
igual	same
diferente	different

diferentes

ocupado

juntos

solo

útil

asustado

ocupado(a)	busy
útil	useful
juntos(as)	together
solo(a)	alone
asustado(a)	frightened
valiente	brave

valiente

descuidado

enfadada

animado

cuidadoso

contenta con

aburrido

descuidado(a)	careless
cuidadoso(a)	careful
enfadado(a)	cross
contento(a) con	pleased with
animado(a)	lively
aburrido(a)	bored, boring

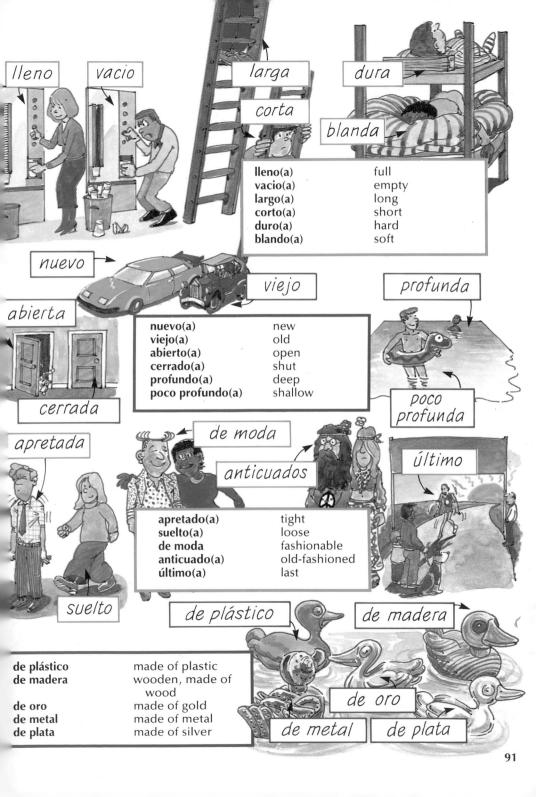

lleno

vacio

larga

dura

corta

blanda

lleno(a)	full
vacio(a)	empty
largo(a)	long
corto(a)	short
duro(a)	hard
blando(a)	soft

nuevo

viejo

profunda

abierta

nuevo(a)	new
viejo(a)	old
abierto(a)	open
cerrado(a)	shut
profundo(a)	deep
poco profundo(a)	shallow

cerrada

poco profunda

apretada

de moda

último

anticuados

apretado(a)	tight
suelto(a)	loose
de moda	fashionable
anticuado(a)	old-fashioned
último(a)	last

suelto

de plástico

de madera

de oro

de metal

de plata

de plástico	made of plastic
de madera	wooden, made of wood
de oro	made of gold
de metal	made of metal
de plata	made of silver

Colors

el color

rojo

amarillo
vivo

azul

rosado
claro

azul marino

blanco

anaranjado

morado
oscuro

negro

verde

gris

apagado

estampado

con lunares

marrón

a rayas

el color	color	vivo(a)	bright
rojo(a)	red	**anaranjado***	orange
rosado(a)	pink	**azul**	blue
claro(a)	pale	**azul marino**	navy blue
blanco(a)	white	**morado(a)**	purple
negro(a)	black	**oscuro(a)**	dark
gris	grey	**verde**	green
apagado(a)	dull	**estampado(a)**	printed
marrón	brown	**con lunares**	spotted
amarillo(a)	yellow	**a rayas**	striped

*The feminine form is **de color naranja**.

In, on, under...

en · debajo de · dentro · sobre · por encima de · fuera · al lado de · cerca de · delante de · detrás de · entre · lejos de · por · hacia · contra · desde · abajo · entre · con · arriba · frente a · sin

en	in	**detrás de**	behind
sobre	on	**contra**	against
debajo de	under	**por**	through
por encima de	over	**entre**	among
dentro	into	**hacia**	to, towards
fuera	out of	**desde**	away from
al lado de	beside	**arriba**	up
entre	between	**abajo**	down
cerca de	near	**frente a**	opposite
lejos de	far away from	**con**	with
delante de	in front of	**sin**	without

Action words

cuchichear

gritar

buscar

esperar

apoyarse en

tener

cuchichear	to whisper
gritar	to shout
buscar	to look for
esperar	to wait for
apoyarse en	to lean on
tener	to hold

llevar

recoger

dejar caer

depositar

| llevar | to carry | recoger | to pick up |
| dejar caer | to drop | depositar | to put down |

tocar

cerrar

abrir

verter

llenar

sacudir

vaciar

tocar	to touch
abrir	to open
cerrar	to close
verter	to pour
llenar	to fill
sacudir	to shake
vaciar	to empty

rasgar

tirar

coger

rasgar	to tear
zurcir	to mend
tirar	to throw
coger	to catch
volcar	to knock over
romper	to break

zurcir

volcar

romper

robar

resbalar

tirar

empujar

escapar

seguir

esconderse

tirar	to pull	escapar	to run away
empujar	to push	seguir	to follow
robar	to steal	esconderse	to hide
resbalar	to slip		

95

Grammar hints

In order to speak Spanish well, you need to learn a bit about the grammar, that is, how you put words together and make sentences. On the next few pages there are some hints on Spanish grammar. Don't worry if you cannot remember them all at first. Try to learn a little grammar at a time and then practice using it.

Nouns

In Spanish all nouns are either masculine or feminine. The word you use for "the" is **el** before a masculine noun and **la** before a feminine noun*:

el vaso	glass
la mesa	table

Most nouns ending in "o" are masculine and those ending in "a" are feminine. Nouns ending in "e" may be masculine or feminine:

la calle	street
el parque	park

Some nouns which describe what a person is or does can be both masculine and feminine:

el amigo	friend (m)
la amiga	friend (f)
el estudiante	student (m)
la estudiante	student (f)
el turista	tourist (m)
la turista	tourist (f)

When they appear in the illustrated section, only the form which matches with the picture is given,

but both the masculine and feminine are given in the word list at the back of the book.

Plurals

When you are talking about more than one thing, the word for "the" is **los** for masculine nouns and **las** for feminine nouns:

los vasos
las mesas

If "the" refers to a group of nouns and one of them is masculine, **los** is used:

los mesas y vasos   the tables and glasses

To make nouns plural, you usually add "s" to those ending in a vowel, and "es" to those ending in a consonant:

la calle	street
las calles	streets
la ciudad	city
las ciudades	cities

a, an, some

The word for "a" is **un** before a masculine noun and **una** before a feminine noun:

un vaso
una mesa

*There are a few exceptions, e.g. **el agua** water, and **el águila** eagle, are feminine.

The word for "some" is **unos** before a masculine plural noun and **unas** before a feminine plural noun:

unos vasos   some glasses
unas mesas   some tables

this, that

"This" is **este** before a masculine noun and **esta** before a feminine noun. The plural, "these", is **estos** before a masculine noun and **estas** before a feminine noun:

este vaso   **estos vasos**
esta mesa   **estas mesas**

"That" is **ese** before a masculine noun and **esa** before a feminine noun. The plural, "those", is **esos** before a masculine noun and **esas** before a feminine noun:

ese vaso   **esos vasos**
esa mesa   **esas mesas**

In Spanish there is another word for "that", **aquel**. **Aquel** is used when you are talking about something that is far away from both you and the person you are speaking to:

aquel vaso   **aquellos vasos**
aquella mesa   **aquellas mesas**

my, your

"My", "your", "his", "her" and so on are called possessive adjectives. In Spanish they change according to whether the noun which follows is singular or plural*:

my	s	pl
(m)	**mi amigo**	**mis amigos**
	my friend	my friends
(f)	**mi hermana**	**mis hermanas**
	my sister	my sisters

your (informal**, s)
tu amigo   **tus amigos**
tu hermana   **tus hermanas**
his/her/its/your (formal**, s)
su amigo   **sus amigos**
su hermana   **sus hermanas**
our
nuestro amigo   **nuestros amigos**
nuestra hermana   **nuestras hermanas**
your (informal**, pl)
vuestro amigo   **vuestros amigos**
vuestra hermana   **vuestras hermanas**
their/your (formal**, pl)
su amigo   **sus amigos**
su hermana   **sus hermanas**

Adjectives

Adjectives are describing words. In Spanish, adjectives usually follow the noun they are describing. They also change their endings depending on whether they are describing a masculine or a feminine noun and whether it is singular or plural. Most adjectives end in "o" in the masculine and this "o" changes to "a" in the feminine:

un vecino simpático   a pleasant neighbor
una película aburrida   a boring film

Adjectives ending in "e" or a consonant don't change in the feminine:

el vaso grande   the big glass
la mesa grande   the big table
el vestido gris   the grey dress
la corbata gris   the grey tie

*"Our" **nuestro** and "your" **vuestro** also change according to whether the noun is masculine or feminine. **See Pronouns on page 98.

The following adjectives showing nationality end in a consonant but do take an "a" in the feminine:

m	f	
alemán	alemana	German
español	española	Spanish
francés	francesa	French
inglés	inglesa	English
irlandés	irlandesa	Irish
holandés	holandesa	Dutch
portugués	portugesa	Portuguese

To make adjectives plural, you add "s" if it ends in a vowel and "es" if it ends in a consonant:

los vecinos simpáticos
las corbatas grises

Comparing adjectives

To compare things, you put **tan... como** (as... as), **más... que** (more... than) and **el, la, los** or **las más** (the most) with an adjective. The adjective agrees in the usual way:

Ella es tan alta como su hermano.
She is as tall as her brother.
Ella es más delgada que yo. She is slimmer than I am.
Soy el más guapo. I am the best looking.

Just as in English, some common adjectives do not add **más** (more) or **el más,** but change completely:

bueno	good
mejor	better
el mejor	the best

malo	bad
peor	worse
el peor	the worst

grande	big
mayor	bigger
el mayor	the biggest

Pronouns

"I", "you", "he", "she" and so on are called personal pronouns. You use them in place of a noun. In Spanish there are several words for "you". **Tú** and **vosotros/as** are informal and are most commonly used. **Usted** and **ustedes** are formal and are used when you are talking to people in authority, strangers or older people. **Usted** and **ustedes** are often written **Vd.** and **Vds.**.

yo	I
tú	you (informal, s)
él	he, it
ella	she, it
usted (Vd.)	you (formal, s)
nosotros/as	we (m/f)
vosotros/as	you (m/f informal, pl)
ellos	they (m)
ellas	they (f)
ustedes (Vds.)	you (formal, pl)

"It" is **él** for a masculine word and **ella** for a feminine word. "They" is **ellos** for masculine words and **ellas** for feminine words. For masculine and feminine words together, you use **ellos.**

Verbs

Spanish verbs (action words) change their endings according to who is doing the action. The pronoun, "I", "you" and so on is often left out because the ending of the verb tells you who is doing the action. Most verbs follow regular patterns of endings. There are three patterns according to whether the verb's infinitive (e.g. in English: "to buy"; "to sew") ends in "ar", "er" or "ir". These are the endings for the present tense:

comprar to buy

compro	I buy, I am buying
compras	you (informal, s) buy
compra	he, she, it buys; you (formal, s) buy
compramos	we buy
compráis	you (informal, pl) buy
compran	they buy; you (formal, pl) buy

coser to sew	**subir** to climb
coso	**subo**
coses	**subes**
cose	**sube**
cosemos	**subimos**
coséis	**subís**
cosen	**suben**

Some of the most common verbs do not follow these patterns in the present tense. They are known as irregular verbs and you need to learn them separately. One of the most common of these is **haber**. **Haber** is a special verb used only for forming the perfect tense (see below right). It is not used by itself. This is the present tense of **haber**:

haber

he
has
ha
hemos
habéis
han

Two other common irregular verbs are **ser** and **estar**. These both mean "to be", but are used in different ways. You use **ser** to describe things that are permanent, or a quality or profession: e.g. "I am Spanish"; "He is tall"; "She is a pianist". **Estar** is used to describe things that can change: e.g. "I am tired"; "It is cold". **Estar** is also used to say where things are: e.g. "The theatre is over there"; "I am here".

Here are the present tenses of **ser** and **estar**:

ser	**estar**
soy	**estoy**
eres	**estás**
es	**está**
somos	**estamos**
sois	**estáis**
son	**están**

You can find other irregular verbs on page 103.

The future tense is used for things you are going to do. It is the same for the three verb types, and it is made by adding these endings to the infinitive:

comprar é
comprar ás
comprar á
comprar emos
comprar éis
comprar án

You use the perfect tense for events which have already happened, ("I have danced" or "I danced", in English). In Spanish you make the perfect tense by putting the present of **haber** with the past participle of the verb. The past participle is made with the stem of the verb (the verb's infinitive less its "ar", "er" or "ir" ending) and a new ending:

infinitive	past participle
compr ar	**compr ado**
cos er	**cos ido**
sub ir	**sub ido**

Here are the perfect tenses of **comprar, coser** and **subir:**

he comprado
has comprado
ha comprado
hemos comprado
habéis comprado
han comprado

he cosido
has cosido
ha cosido
hemos cosido
habéis cosido
han cosido

he subido
has subido
ha subido
hemos subido
habéis subido
han subido

Stem-changing verbs

There is a group of verbs in Spanish in which the last vowel in the stem changes in the present tense (except in the "we" and "you" forms). Verbs of this sort are called stem-changing verbs and you need to learn which they are. There is a list of the most common ones on page 102. In verbs that have "e" as the last vowel in the stem, the "e" changes to "ie", or in a few cases to "i". In verbs that have "o" as the last vowel in their stem, the "o" changes to "ue".

Here are the present tenses of **cerrar** which has an "e" that changes to "ie", **seguir** with an "e" that changes to "i", and **encontrar** with an "o" that changes to "ue".

cerrar (ie)   to shut

cierro
cierras
cierra
cerramos
cerráis
cierran

seguir (i)   to follow

sigo*
sigues
sigue
seguimos
seguís
siguen

encontrar (ue)   to find

encuentro
encuentras
encuentra
encontramos
encontráis
encuentran

*The "u" in **seguir** makes the "g" hard. It is not needed here as "g" is also hard before "a" or "o".

Reflexive verbs

Verbs which have **se** at the end of the infinitive are called reflexive verbs. These verbs usually involve doing something to yourself (e.g. in English: "to wash oneself"), but you will find that far more verbs can be reflexive in Spanish than in English.

lavarse	to wash oneself
peinarse	to comb one's hair
afeitarse	to shave
levantarse	to get up
dormirse	to fall asleep

Se means "self" and changes according to who is doing the action (as it does in English):

yo me lavo	I wash myself
tú te lavas	you (informal, s) wash yourself
él, ella se lava	he, she washes him/herself
usted se lava	you (formal, s) wash yourself
nosotros nos lavamos	we wash ourselves
vosotros os laváis	you (informal, pl) wash yourselves
ellos, ellas se lavan	they (m/f) wash themselves
ustedes se lavan	you (formal, pl) wash yourselves

Negatives

To make a negative in Spanish, you put **no** before the whole verb. If the verb is reflexive, **no** goes before the reflexive pronoun (**me, te, se** etc):

No hablamos inglés. We do not speak English.
No ha pagado. He has not paid.
No se lava las manos. She isn't washing her hands.
No se han bañado ayer. They didn't go swimming yesterday.

Object pronouns

An object pronoun is a word which is used to replace a noun that is the object of a verb:

Yo prefiero el queso. I prefer cheese.
Yo lo prefiero. I prefer it.

These are the object pronouns in Spanish:

me	me
te	you (informal, s)
lo	him, it
la	her, it
lo, la	you (formal m/f)
nos	us (m/f)
os	you (informal, m/f)
los	them (m)
las	them (f)
los, las	you (formal, pl m/f)

In Spanish you put the object pronoun just before the verb. If the verb is reflexive, the object pronoun goes after the reflexive pronoun.

Lo busco. I am looking for it.
No lo encuentro. I can't find it.
Lo he comprado. I have bought it.
Me lavo las manos. I am washing my hands.
Me las lavo. I am washing them.

Questions

In Spanish you can make a question simply by raising your voice at the end of a sentence:

¿Quieres otra cerveza? You like another beer?/ Would you like another beer?
¿No has empezado aún? Haven't you started yet?
¿Lo has perdido? Have you lost it?

When a question is written down, as well as ending with a question mark, it starts with an upside down question mark. (Note that Spanish exclamation marks are used in the same way.)

Below are some common question words. When you use these, you put the subject after the whole verb (but remember, if the subject is "I", "you"etc, it is usually left out):

¿Cómo...? How...?
¿Cómo has hecho eso? How did you do that?
¿Cuándo...? When...?
¿Cuándo es la fiesta? When is the party?
¿Cuánto...? How much...?
¿Cuánto es esto? How much is this?
¿Dónde...? Where...?
¿Dónde has estado? Where have you been?
¿Qué...? What...?
¿Qué hace Pablo? What is Pablo doing?
¿Quién...? Who...?
¿Quién ha llegado primero? Who got here first?
¿Por qué? Why...?
¿Por qué no nos encontramos luego? Why don't we meet later?

Stem-changing verbs

Here are two lists of verbs which change the last vowel of their stem in the present tense.

The verbs in the first list either have an "e" that changes to "ie" as in **cerrar**, or an "o" that changes to "ue" as in **encontrar** (see page 100):

acostarse	to go to bed
cerrar	to shut
cocer	to cook
colgar	to hang
contar	to tell a story, to count
costar	to cost
deshelar	to thaw
despertarse	to wake up
devolver	to give back
divertirse	to enjoy oneself
empezar	to begin
encender	to switch on, to light
encontrar	to find
envolver	to wrap up
fregar	to rub, to scrub
helar	to freeze
jugar (u becomes ue)	to play
llover	to rain
morder	to bite
morir	to die
mover	to move
negarse	to refuse
nevar	to snow
oler (o becomes hue)	to smell
pensar	to think
perder	to lose
preferir	to prefer
probar	to try, to prove
querer	to like, to love

recordar	to remember, to remind
sentarse	to sit down
sentirse	to feel
soñar	to dream
temblar	to tremble, to shake
torcer	to twist
verter	to pour, to spill
volar	to fly
volcar	to knock over, to overturn
volver	to return

The verbs in this list have an "e" as their last stem vowel which changes to "i", and they form their present tense in the same way as **seguir** (see page 100):

corregir	to correct
despedirse	to say goodbye
pedir	to ask for
reír	to laugh
reñir	to scold
repetir	to repeat
seguir	to follow
sonreír	to smile
vestirse	to dress

Irregular verbs

Here are the present tenses of some common irregular verbs, together with the **yo** form of the future and perfect tenses. Try to learn these verbs as you will probably need to use them quite frequently when you are speaking Spanish.

decir   to say

digo
dices
dice
decimos
decís
dicen

future: **diré**
perfect: **he dicho**

hacer   to do, to make

hago
haces
hace
hacemos
hacéis
hacen

future: **haré**
perfect: **he hecho**

ir   to go

voy
vas
va
vamos
vais
van

future: **iré**
perfect: **he ido**

oír to hear

oigo
oyes
oye
oímos
oís
oyen

future: **oiré**
perfect: **he oído**

poder to be able to

puedo
puedes
puede
podemos
podéis
pueden

future: **podré**
perfect: **he podido**

poner to put

pongo
pones
pone
ponemos
ponéis
ponen

future: **pondré**
perfect: **he puesto**

querer to want

quiero
quieres
quiere
queremos
queréis
quieren

future: **querré**
perfect: **he querido**

reír to laugh

río
ríes
ríe
reímos
reís
ríen

future: **reiré**
perfect: **he reído**

saber to know

sé
sabes
sabe
sabemos
sabéis
saben

future: **sabré**
perfect: **he sabido**

salir to go out

salgo
sales
sale
salimos
salís
salen

future: **saldré**
perfect: **he salido**

ser to be

soy
eres
es
somos
sois
son

future: **seré**
perfect: **he sido**

tener   to have, to hold

tengo
tienes
tiene
tenemos
tenéis
tienen

future: **tendré**
perfect: **he tenido**

valer   to be worth

valgo
vales
vale
valemos
valéis
valen

future: **valdré**
perfect: **he valido**

venir   to come

vengo
vienes
viene
venimos
venís
vienen

future: **vendré**
perfect: **he venido**

ver   to see

veo
ves
ve
vemos
veis
ven

future: **veré**
perfect: **he visto**

The following verbs are only irregular in the first person singular of the present tense (e.g. "I fall" or "I am falling"); the rest of the verb is regular:

caer	to fall
caigo	I fall
dar	to give
doy	I give
estar	to be
estoy	I am
traer	to bring
traigo	I bring

Phrase explainer

Throughout the illustrated section of this book, there are useful short phrases and everyday expressions. You may find these easier to remember if you understand the different words that make them up.

This section lists the expressions under the page number where they appeared (although those whose word for word meaning is like the English have been left out). After reminding you of the suggested English equivalent, it shows you how they break down and, wherever possible, gives you the literal translations of the words involved.* Any grammatical terms used are explained in the grammar hints.

page 4
- **¡Hasta pronto!** See you later:
hasta=until; **pronto**=soon.
- **¿Qué tal?** How are you?
¿qué?=what/how?; **tal**=such. Common expression, close to "How are things?"
- **Muy bien, ¡gracias!** Very well, thank you:
muy=very; **bien**=well; **gracias**=thanks.

page 5
- **De acuerdo.** I agree./Agreed!
de=of; **el acuerdo**=agreement.
- **¿Cómo te llamas?** What's your name?
¿cómo?=how?; **te llamas**=you call yourself.
- **Me llamo...** My name is...
- **El se llama...** His name is...
llamarse=to call oneself. In Spanish, this reflexive verb is used for saying your name.
- **¿Cuántos años tienes?** How old are you?
¿cuántos?=how many?; **años**=years; **tienes**=you have/hold.
- **Tengo diecinueve años.** I'm nineteen:
tengo=I hold/have; **diecinueve**=nineteen.

page 12
- **Es mi casa.** This is where I live:
es=it is; **mi casa**=my house.

page 18
- **¡Atención al perro!** Beware of the dog:
la atención=care; **al perro** is short for **a el perro**=to/at the dog.

page 20
- **¡Buenos días!** Good morning:
buenos=good (m pl); **días**=days (note that **día** is masculine despite its "a" ending).

page 25
- **¡Hasta mañana!** Good-night:
hasta=until; **la mañana**=morning/tomorrow.
- **¡Que duermas bien!** Sleep well:
que duermas=that you should sleep; **bien**=well.

page 26
- **Ya está.** It's ready:
ya=already; **está**=it is.
- **¡Sírvete!** Help yourself:
sírvete=serve yourself. (**sirve**=serve; **te**=yourself. Note that the pronoun and verb are joined up: this is because unstressed pronouns are pronounced as part of the preceding verb, and the convention is to write them like this).
- **¡Que aproveche!** Enjoy your meal:
=that you should make full use (of). This is a polite phrase you say to people who are about to eat.
- **Está muy rico.** It tastes good:
está=it is; **muy**=very; **rico**=rich/delicious.

page 31
- **¡Riquísimo!** Delicious!
=very, very rich/delicious, most delicious.

page 37
- **¿Qué van a tomar?** What would you like?
¿qué?=what?; **van**=are you (pl) going; **a**=to; **tomar**=take.
- **¿Está incluido el servicio?** Is service included?
está=is; **incluido**=included; **el servicio**=service.

*Literal meanings of Spanish words are introduced by the sign =.

- **El servicio no está incluido.** Service is not included:
no=not.

page 43
- **¿Cuánto es todo?** How much do I owe you?
¿cuánto?=how many/how much?; **es**=(it) is; **todo**=all.
- **Todo es...** That will be...
e.g. **Todo es cien pesetas**=That will be 100 pesetas.

page 44
- **No es caro.** It's good value:
no=not; **es**=it is; **caro**=dear/expensive.
- **Es algo caro.** It's expensive:
algo=somewhat.
- **¿Qué desea?** Can I help you?
¿qué?=what?; **desea**=you desire.
- **¿Cuánto cuesta...?** How much is...?
- **Cuesta...** It costs...
¿Cuánto?=how much/how many?; **cuesta**=it costs.

page 48
- **¡Dígame!** Hello!
diga=say; **me**=to me; (note that the pronoun and verb are joined up: see **¡Sírvete!** page 26.) **¡Dígame!** is used for "hello" on the telephone, but also means "what do you want?" when you want someone to tell you something.
- **¿Quién habla?** Who's speaking?
¿quién?=who?; **habla**=he/she speaks.
- **Soy Juanita.** It's Juanita:
soy=I am; **Juanita**=a girl's name.
- **Te llamo más tarde.** I'll call you back:
te=to you; **llamo**=I call; **más**=more; **tarde**=late.
- **la llamada de urgencia** 911 call:
la llamada=the call; **de**=of; **urgencia**=urgency/emergency.

page 49
- **Muy señor mío:/Estimada señora:**
Dear Sir/Madam:
muy=very; **señor**=Sir/Mr; **mío (m)**=my; **estimada (f)**=esteemed; **señora**=Madam/Mrs. This is how you begin a formal letter.

- **Le saluda atentamente** Yours faithfully:
le=to you (formal, s);**saluda**=he/she greets, salutes; **atentamente**=attentively, with attention. This is how you end a formal letter.
- **Me encantó tener noticias tuyas.** It was lovely to hear from you:
me=to me; **encantó**=enchanted; **tener**=to have; **noticias**=news; **tuyas (f pl)**=your.
- **Pasándolo muy bien** Having a lovely time:
pasándolo (pasando lo)=passing/spending it (verb and pronoun are written together: see **¡Sírvete!** page 26); **muy**=very; **bien**=well.
- **Deseando verte pronto** Look forward to seeing you soon:
deseando=desiring/wishing; **verte (ver te)**=to see you; **pronto**=soon.
- **Recado urgente** Urgent message:
recado=message; **urgente**=urgent.

page 50
- **¿Por dónde está...?** Which way is...?
por=by; **¿dónde?**=where?; **está**=(it) is.
- **¿A qué distancia está...?** How far is...?
a=at/to; **¿qué?**=what?; **distancia**=distance.

page 52
- **dirección única** one way:
dirección=direction; **única (f s)**=only/sole.
- **dirección prohibida** no entry:
prohibida (f s)=prohibited.
- **¡Prohibido el estacionamiento!** No parking:
el estacionamiento=the parking.

page 54
- **El tren para/desde...** The train to/from...
el tren=the train; **para**=for; **desde**=from.
- **el tren TALGO** inter-city train:
TALGO stands for **tren articulado ligero Goicoechea Oriol**=train articulated light, and the last two words are the name of the engineer who designed the train.
- **Prohibido fumar** No smoking:
prohibido=prohibited; **fumar**=to smoke.

page 56
- **nada que declarar**   nothing to declare:
nada=nothing; **que**=that/for; **declarar**=to declare.

page 57
- **la tienda libre de impuestos**   duty free shop:
la tienda=the shop; **libre**=free; **de**=of; **impuestos**=taxes.
- **¡Abrocharse el cinturón!**   Fasten your seatbelts:
abrocharse=to fasten oneself up (the infinitive is used to give a polite order); **el cinturón**=the belt.

page 58
- **hacer la maleta**   to pack:
hacer=to make; **la maleta**=the suitcase.
- **visitar los lugares de interés**   to sightsee:
visitar=to visit; **los lugares**=the places; **de**=of; **interés**=interest.

page 76
- **Dentro**   In:
=inside.
- **Fuera**   Out:
=outside.

page 78
- **¡Felicidades!**   Congratulations!
=felicitations/happinesses. This is what you say for someone's birthday, wedding, promotion...

page 79
- **¡Felices Pascuas!**   Merry Christmas:
felices (f pl)=happy/merry; **Pascuas (de Navidad)**=Christmas (**Pascua** is a religious festival in the Catholic Church. The three main **Pascuas** are **Pascuas de Navidad**=Christmas, **Pascuas de Resurrección**=Easter, and **Pascuas de Pentecostés**=Whitsun. However ¡**Felices Pascuas!** is mostly used at Christmas. **Navidad**=nativity, birth).
- **¡Muchas gracias!**   Thank you:
muchas (f pl)=many; **gracias**=thanks.
- **¡Feliz Año!**   Happy New Year:
feliz=happy; **año**=year.

page 82
- **Amanece.**   It is getting light:
amanecer=to dawn, to get light.
- **Es de día.**   It is light:
es=it is; **de**=of; **día**=day.
- **Oscurece.**   It is getting dark:
oscurecer=to get/grow dark.
- **Es de noche.**   It is dark:
es=it is; **de**=of; **noche**=night.

page 83
- **¿Qué hora es?**   What time is it?
¿qué?=what?; **hora**=hour; **es**=it is/is it.
- **Es la una.**   It is 1 o'clock:
es=it is; **la una (f)**=the one (**la una** is feminine as **hora**=hour is unstated but understood).
- **Son las tres.**   It is 3 o'clock:
son=they are; **las (f pl)**=the; **tres**=three.
- **las diez menos cuarto**   a quarter to 10:
las=the; **diez**=ten; **menos**=minus; **cuarto**=quarter.
- **las diez y cinco/cuarto/media**   five/a quarter/half past 10:
las=the; **diez**=ten; **y**=and; **cinco**=five; **cuarto**=quarter; **media**=half.
- **las ocho de la mañana/noche**   8 a.m./p.m.:
las=the; **ocho**=eight; **de**=of; **la mañana**=morning; **la noche**=night.

page 85
- **Hace bueno.**   It's fine:
hace=it does/makes; **bueno**=good.
- **Brilla el sol.**   The sun is shining:
brilla=it shines; **el sol**=the sun (the subject follows the verb for stylistic reasons: you could also say **el sol brilla**).
- **Tengo calor.**   I'm hot:
tengo=I have; **el calor**=heat (**calor** is occasionally used with the feminine article **la**).
- **Hace viento/frío**   It's windy/cold:
hace=it does/makes; **el viento**=wind; **el frío**=cold.
- **Hay niebla.**   It's foggy:
hay=there is (**hay** can also be used in the plural as "there are", and is a very common expression); **la niebla**=fog.

English-Spanish word list

Here you will find all the Spanish words, phrases and expressions from the illustrated section of this book listed in English alphabetical order. Wherever useful, phrases and expressions are cross-referenced, and the words they are made up from are included in the list.

Following each Spanish term, you will find its pronunciation in italics. To pronounce Spanish properly, you need to listen to a Spanish person speaking. This pronunciation guide will give you an idea as to how to pronounce new words and act as a reminder to words you have heard spoken.

Remember that
- the Spanish ñ is like the *ni* sound in *onion*
- *v* is like an English *b*
- *ll* is said like *y* in *yes* but with a hint of an *l* before it
- *g* (when it precedes an *i* or an *e*) and *j* sound like *ch* in the Scottish *loch* (a guttural *h*)
- *c* (when it precedes an *i* or an *e*), *d* (when it is on the end of a syllable) and *z* are like *th* in English
- *h* is not pronounced.

When using the pronunciation hints in italics, read them as if they were English "words", but bear in mind the following points:

- it is important in Spanish to stress the correct part of the word: the syllable you should stress is shown in CAPITAL letters
- *a* represents the *a* sound in *happen*
- *e* is like the *e* in *felt*
- *ee* like *ee* in *keen*
- *o* like *o* in *hot*
- *oo* like *oo* in *boot*
- *ch* like *ch* in *loch*
- *ly* like the *ly* sound in *Delia*
- *rrr* represents the Spanish rolled *r*. To say it, make a trilling sound with the tip of your tongue placed behind your top teeth.

A

English	Spanish	Pronunciation
to accelerate	acelerar	*atheleRAR*
actor	el actor	*el akTOR*
actress	la actriz	*la akTREETH*
to add	hacer cuentas	*aTHER KWENtas*
address	las señas	*lass SSENyas*
adhesive bandage	el esparadrapo	*el essparaDRApo*
advertisement	el anuncio	*el aNOONtheeyo*
Africa	África	*Afreeka*
afternoon, evening	la tarde	*la TARde*
against	contra	*KONtra*
age	la edad	*la eDAth*
I agree, agreed	de acuerdo	*de aKWERdo*
air steward	el camarero	*el kamaREro*
airmail	por avión	*por aBYONN*
airplane	el avión	*el aBYONN*
airport	el aeropuerto	*el aeroPWERto*
aisle	la nave	*la NAbe*
alarm clock	el despertador	*el despertaDOR*
alone	solo(a)	*ssOlo(a)*
alphabet	el alfabeto	*el alfaBEto*
ambulance	la ambulancia	*la ambooLANtheeya*
among	entre	*ENtre*
anchor	el ancla (f)	*el ANGkla*
and	y	*ee*
animal	el animal	*el aneeMAL*
ankle	el tobillo	*el toBEELyo*
to answer	contestar	*kontessTAR*
to answer the telephone	kontestar al teléfono	*kontessTAR al teLEfono*
apartment	el piso	*el PEEsso*
block of apartments	la casa de pisos	*la KAssa de PEEssoss*
apple	la manzana	*la manTHAna*
apple tree	el manzano	*el manTHAno*
apricot	el albaricoque	*el albareeKOKe*
April	abril	*aBREEL*
architect (m)	el arquitecto	*el arkeeTEKto*
architect (f)	la arquitecta	*la arkeeTEKta*
area code	la cifra regional	*la THEEfra rrecheeyoNAL*
arm	el brazo	*el BRAtho*
armchair	el sillón	*el sseelYON*
Arrivals	Llegadas	*lyeGAdass*
art gallery	la galería de arte	*la galeREEya de ARte*
article (in newspaper)	el artículo	*el arTEEkulo*
to ask, to ask a question	preguntar	*pregunTAR*
to ask the way	preguntar el camino	*pregunTAR el kaMEEno*
to fall asleep	dormirse	*dorMEERsse*
at the beach	en la playa	*en la PLAya*
athletics	el atletismo	*el adleTEEzmo*
Atlantic Ocean	el Atlántico	*el adLANteeko*
attic	el desván	*el dezBAN*
audience	el público	*el POObleeko*
August	agosto	*aGOSSto*
aunt	la tía	*la TEEya*
Australia	Australia	*aoossTRAleeya*
autumn	el otoño	*el oTONyo*
away from	desde	*dezde*

B

baby	el bebé	el beBE
back	la espalda	la essPALda
to do back-stroke	hacer la braza de espalda	athER la BRAtha de essPALda
backwards	hacia atrás	Atheeya aTRASS
bag	la bolsita	la bolSSEEta
bait	el cebo	el THEbo
baker, baker's	el panadero	el panaDEro
balcony	el balcón	el balKONN
with balcony	con balcón	kon balKONN
bald	calvo(a)	KALbo(a)
to be bald	ser calvo	sser KALbo
ball	la pelota	la peLOta
ballet	el ballet	el baLE
ballet dancer (m)	el bailarín	el baeelaREEN
ballet dancer (f)	la bailarina	la baeelaREEna
balloon	el globo	el GLObo
banana	el plátano	el PLAtano
bandage	la venda	la BENda
bangs	el flequillo	el fleKEELyo
bank (river)	la orilla	la OREELya
bank	el banco	el BANGko
bank manager	el gerente del banco	el cheRENte del BANGko
barefoot	descalzo(a)	dessKALtho(a)
a bargain	una ganga (f)	OOna GANGga
to bark	ladrar	laDRAR
barn	el granero	el graNEro
barrier	la barrera	la baRRREra
basement	el sótano	el SSOtano
basket (large)	el cesto	el THESSto
basket, shopping basket	la cesta	la THESSta
to have a bath	bañarse	banYARsse
to run a bath	poner el baño	poNER el BANyo
bathmat	la esterita de baño	la essteREEta de BANyo
bathrobe	el albornoz	el alborNOTH
bathroom	el cuarto de baño	el KWARto de BANyo
bathtub	el baño	el BANyo
to be	ser	sser
to be	estar	essTAR
to be born	nacer	naTHER
to be called, to be named	llamarse	lyaMARsse
to be fond of	tenerle cariño a	teNERle kaREENyo a
to be frozen	estar helado(a)	essTAR eLAdo(a)
to be happy	ser feliz	sser feLEETH
to be hungry	tener hambre	teNER AMbre
to be late	llegar tarde	lyeGAR TARde
to be on time	llegar a la hora	lyeGAR a la Ora
to be on time	llegar a tiempo	lyeGAR a TYEMpo
to be seasick	marearse	mareARsse
to be sick, vomit	vomitar	bomeeTAR
to be sleepy	estar cansado(a)	essTAR kanSSAdo(a)
to be thirsty	tener sed	teNER seth
beach	la playa	la PLAya
at/on the beach	en la playa	en la PLAya
beak	el pico	el PEEko
green beans	la judía verde	la chooDEEya BERde
kidney beans	las judías	las chooDEEyas
beard	la barba	la BARba
to have a beard	tener barba	teNER BARba
bed	la cama	la KAma
to go to bed	acostarse	akossTARsse
bedroom	el dormitorio	el dormeeTOReeyo
bedside table	la mesilla de noche	la meSSEELya de NOTshe
bedspread	la colcha	la KOLLtsha
bedtime	la hora de acostarse	la Ora de akossTARsse
bee	la abeja	la aBEcha
beer	la cerveza	la therBEtha
behind	detrás de	deTRASS de
Belgium	Bélgica	BELLcheeka
bell	la campana	la kamPAna
doorbell	el timbre	el TEEMbre
to belong to	pertenecer a	perteneTHER a
belt	el cinturón	el theentooRONN
safety belt, seatbelt	el cinturón de seguridad	el theentooRONN de ssegooreedath
bench	el banco	el BANGko
beside	al lado de	al LAdo de
better	mejor	meCHOR
to feel better	sentirse mejor	ssenTEERsse meCHOR
between	entre	ENtre
Beware of the dog	¡Atención al perro!	atenTHYON al PErrro
bicycle	la bicicleta	la beetheeKLEta
big	grande	GRANde
bill	la cuenta	la KWENta
biology	la biología	la beeoloCHEEya
bird	el pájaro	el PAcharo
birth	el nacimiento	el naceeMYENto
birthday	el cumpleaños	el koompleaANyos
birthday card	la tarjeta	la tarCHEta
bitter	agrio(a)	Agreeyo(a)
black	negro(a)	NEgro(a)
blackbird	el mirlo	el MEERlo
blackboard	el encerado	el entheRAdo
block of apartments	la casa de pisos	la KAssa de PEEssoss
blond	rubio(a)	RRROObeeyo(a)
blond hair	el pelo rubio	el PElo RRROObeeyo
blouse	la blusa	la BLOOssa
blue	azul	aTHOOL
to board the plane	abordar el avión	aborDAR el abYONN
board game	los juegos de tablero	loss CHWEgoss de taBLEro
boarding house	la pensión	la penSSYON
boat, small boat	la barca	la BARka
to travel by boat	ir en barco	eer en BARko
body	el cuerpo	el KWERpo
book	el libro	el LEEbro
picture book	el libro de imágenes	el LEEbro de eeMAcheness
booked up, fully booked	está completo	essTA komPLEto
bookshop	la librería	la leebreREEya
bookshop and stationer's	la librería y la papelería	la leebreREEya ee la papeleREEya
boots	las botas	lass BOtass
rubber boots	las botas de goma	lass BOtass de GOma
bored	aburrido(a)	abooRRREEdo(a)
boring	aburrido(a)	abooRRREEdo(a)
to be born	nacer	naTHER
boss (m)	el jefe	el CHEfe
boss (f)	la jefa	la CHEfa
bottle	la botella	la boTELya

bouquet	el ramo de flores	el RRRAmo de FLOress
boutique	la tienda de modas	la TYENda de MOdass
bowl	el tazón	el taTHON
bowl (for goldfish)	el cuenco de cristal	el KWENko de kreessTAL
box office	la taquilla	la taKEELya
boy	el niño	el NEENyo
bra	el sostén	el ssossTEN
bracelet	la pulsera	la poolSSEra
braids	trenzas (f.pl)	TRENthass
branch	la rama	la RRRAma
brave	valiente	balYENte
Bravo!	¡Bravo!	BRAbo
bread	el pan	el pan
break (at school)	el descanso	el dessKANsso
to break	romper	rrromPER
to break your leg	romperse la pierna	rrromPERsse la PYERna
breakdown (vehicle)	la avería	la abeREEya
to have a breakdown	tener una avería	teNER oona abeREEya
breakfast	el desayuno	el dessaYOOno
to do breast-stroke	hacer la braza de pecho	aTHER la BRAtha de PETsho
bride	la novia	la NObeeya
bridegroom	el novio	el NObeeyo
bridge	el puente	el PWENte
bright	vivo(a)	BEEbo(a)
to bring up	criar	KREEar
broad	ancho(a)	ANTsho(a)
brooch	el prendedor	el prendeDOR
brother	el hermano	el erMAno
brown	marrón	maRRRON
brown hair	el pelo castaño	el PElo kassTANyo
bruise	la contusión	la kontooSYON
brush (for painting)	el pincel	el peenTHEL
brush	el cepillo	el thePEELyo
toothbrush	el cepillo de dientes	el thePEELyo de DYENtess
to brush your hair	cepillarse el pelo	thepeelYARsse el PElo
Brussels sprout	la col de Bruselas	la kol de brooSSElass
bucket	el cubito	el kooBEEto
buffet car	el coche-restaurante	el KOTshe rrrestaooRANte
builder	el albañil	el albanYEEL
building	el edificio	el edeeFEEtheeyo
bulb (plant)	el bulbo	el BOOLbo
bunch of flowers	el manojo de flores	el maNOcho de FLOress
burn	la quemadura	la kemaDOOra
to burst out laughing	echarse a reír	etSHARSSE a rrreEER
bus	el bus	el BOOS
bus stop	la parada de autobuses	la paRAda de aootoBOOssess
to take the bus	coger el bus	koCHER el BOOSS
bush	el arbusto	el arBOOSSto
busy	ocupado(a)	okooPAdo(a)
bustling	yendo y viniendo	YENdo e beenYENdo
butcher	el carnicero	el karneeTHEro
butter	la mantequilla	la manteKEELya
butterfly	la mariposa	la mareePOssa
button	el botón	el boTON

| to buy | comprar | komPRAR |
| by return mail | a vuelta de correo | a BWELta de KORRREo |

C

cabbage	la col	la kol
cabin	el camarote	el kamaROte
cage	la jaula	la CHAOOla
cake	la torta	la TORta
cake shop	la pastelería	la passteleREEya
to calculate	hacer cuentas	aTHER KWENtass
calculator	la calculadora	la kalkoolaDOra
calendar	el calendario	el kalenDAreeyo
calf	la ternera	la terNEra
camel	el camello	el kaMELyo
camera	la máquina fotográfica	la MAkeena fotoGRAfeeka
to camp, to go camping	ir de camping	eer de KAMpeeng
camper	la caravana	la karaBAna
camping stove	el infiernillo	el eenfyerNEELyo
campsite	el camping	el KAMpeeng
can	el bote	el BOte
Can I help you?	¿Qué desea?	ke deSSEya
Canada	el Canadá	el KanaDA
canary	el canario	el kaNAreeyo
candle	la vela	la BEla
canned food	los productos en lata	loss proDOOKtoss en LAta
canoe	la canoa	la kaNOa
cap	la gorra	la GOrrra
capital letter	la mayúscula	la maYOOSSkoola
to capsize	volcarse	bolKARsse
captain	el capitán	el kapeeTAN
car	el auto	el AOOto
car-park	el aparcamiento	el aparkaMYENto
card	la tarjeta	la tarCHEta
postcard	la tarjeta postal	la tarCHEta posTAL
credit card	la tarjeta de crédito	la tarCHEta de KREdeeto
card (playing card)	la carta	la KARta
to play cards	jugar a las cartas	chooGAR a lass KARtass
cardigan	la chaqueta de punto	la tshaKEta de POOnto
careful	cuidadoso(a)	kweedaDOsso(a)
careless	descuidado(a)	dessskweeDAdo(a)
caretaker (m)	el portero	el porTEro
caretaker (f)	la portera	la porTEra
cargo, load	la carga	la KARga
carnation	el clavel	el klaBEL
carol	el villancico	el beelyanTHEEko
carpet, rug	la alfombra	la alFOMbra
wall-to-wall carpet	la moqueta	la moKEta
to carry	llevar	lyeBAR
carrot	la zanahoria	la thanaOReeya
cashier (m)	el cajero	el kaCHEro
cashier (f)	la cajera	la kaCHEra
cassette	el cassette	el kaSSET
cassette recorder	la grabadora	la grabaDOra
cat	el gato	el GAto
to catch	coger	koCHER
to catch a fish	coger un pez	koCHER oon peth
to catch the train	coger el tren	koCHER el tren
cathedral	la catedral	la kateDRAL
cauliflower	la coliflor	la koleeFLOR
to celebrate	celebrar	theleBRAR

cellar	el sótano	el SSOtano
cello	el violoncelo	el beeolonTHELo
to play the cello	tocar el violoncelo	toKAR el beeolonTHElo
cemetery	el cementerio	el themenTEreeyo
centimeter	el centímetro	el thenTEEmetro
chair	la silla	la SSEELya
chairlift	la silla de ascenso	la SSEELya de assTHENsso
chalk	la tiza	la TEEtha
change	el cambio	el KAMbeeyo
Have you any small change?	¿Tiene cambio?	TYEene KAMbeeyo
to change money	cambiar dinero	kambeeAR deeNEro
channel (TV and radio)	la cadena	la kaDEna
to chase	perseguir	persseGEER
to chat	charlar	tsharLAR
check	el cheque	el TSHEke
to write a check	hacer un cheque	aTHER un TSHEke
check-book	la chequera	la tsheKEra
to play checkers	jugar a las damas	chooGAR a lass DAmass
check-in	la recepción	la rrrethep-THYONN
checkout	la salida de caja	la ssaLEEda de KAcha
cheek	la mejilla	la meCHEELya
cheerful	alegre	aLEgre
cheese	el queso	el KEsso
chemistry	la química	la KEEmeeka
cherry	la cereza	la theREtha
to play chess	jugar al ajedrez	chooGAR al acheDRETH
chest	el pecho	el PEtsho
chick peas	los garbanzos	loss garBANthoss
chicken	el pollo	el POLyo
child	el hijo	el EEcho
childhood	la niñez	la neenYETH
chimney	la chimenea	la tsheemeNEya
chin	la barbilla	la barBEELya
China	China	TSHEEna
chocolate	el chocolate	el tshokoLAte
choir	el coro	el koro
Christmas	las Navidades	lass nabeeDAdess
Christmas Day	el Día de Navidad	el DEEya de nabeeDATH
Merry Christmas	¡Felices Pascuas!	feLEEthess PASSkwass
Christmas tree	el árbol de Navidad	el ARbol de nabeeDATH
chrysanthemum	el crisantemo	el kreessanTEmo
church	la iglesia	la eeGLEsseeya
circle	el círculo	el THEERkoolo
city	la capital	la kapeeTAL
to clap	aplaudir	aplaooDEER
classroom	la clase	la KLAsse
claw	la garra	la GArrra
clean	limpio(a)	LEEMpyo(a)
to clean your teeth	limpiarse los dientes	leempeeARsse loss deeENtess
climate	el clima	el KLEEma
to climb	trepar	trePAR
to climb (mountain climbing)	escalar	esskaLAR
to climb a tree	trepar un árbol	trePAR oon ARbol
climber	el alpinista	el alpeeNEESSta
clock	el reloj	el rrreLOCH

alarm clock	el despertador	el desspertaDOR
to close	cerrar	theRRRAR
clothes, clothing	la ropa	la RRROpa
clothes line	la cuerda de la ropa	la KWERda de la RRROpa
clothes pin	la pinza	la PEENtha
cloud	la nube	la NOObe
coat	el abrigo	el abREEgo
coatroom	el guardarropa	el gwardaRRROpa
cod	el bacalao	el bakaLAO
coffee	el café	el kaFE
coffee-pot	la cafetera	la kafeTEra
coin	la moneda	la moNEda
cold	frío(a)	FREEyo(a)
It's cold.	Hace frío.	Athe FREEyo
cold water	el agua (f) fría	el Agwa FREEya
to have a cold	tener un resfriado	teNER oon rrressfreeYAdo
to collect	coleccionar	kolektheeyoNAR
to collect stamps	coleccionar sellos	kolektheeyoNAR SSELyoss
collection	la colección	la kolekTHYON
collection times (post)	las horas de recogida	lass Orass de rrrekoCHEEda
collision	el choque	el TSHoke
color	el color	el koLOR
comb	el peine	el PEYne
to comb your hair	peinarse	peyNARsse
comic (book)	el tebeo	el teBEyo
complexion	la tez	la teth
computer	la computadora	la kompootaDOra
computer studies	la informática	la eenforMAteeka
condiments	las especias	lass essPEtheyass
conductor (orchestra) (m)	el director de orquesta	el deerekTOR de orKESSta
conductor (orchestra) (f)	la directora de orquesta	la deerektora de orKESSta
cone	el cono	el KOno
to congratulate	felicitar	feleetheeTAR
Congratulations!	¡Felicidades!	feleetheeDAdess
continent	el continente	el konteeNENte
to cook	guisar	geeSSAR
cookie	la galleta	la galYEta
corner	la esquina	la essKEEna
to cost	costar	kossTAR
It costs…	Cuesta…	KWEssta
cottage	la casita	la kaSSEEta
cotton, made of cotton	de algodón	de algoDONN
counter	el mostrador	el mosstraDOR
country	el país	el paEESS
countryside	el campo	el KAMpo
course	el curso	el KOORsso
cousin (m)	el primo	el PREEmo
cousin (f)	la prima	la PREEma
cow	la vaca	la BAka
cowshed	el establo	el essTAblo
crab	el cangrejo	el kanGREcho
to crawl, to do the crawl	hacer el crol	aTHER el krol
crayon	el lápiz de color	el LApeez de koLOR
cream	la nata	la NAta
credit card	la tarjeta de crédito	la tarCHEta de KREdeeto
crew	la tripulación	la treepoolaTHYON
crib	la cuna	la KOOna

cross, angry	enfadado(a)	enfaDAdo(a)	to dig	cavar	kaBAR
to cross the street	atraversar la calle	atrabeSSAR la KALye	dining rom	el comedor	el komeDOR
crossing (sea)	la travesía	la trabeSSEEya	dinner	la comida	la koMEEda
crowd	el grupo de gente	el GROOpo de CHENte	director (f)	la directora	la deerekTORA
			director (m)	el director	el deerekTOR
to cry	llorar	lyoRAR	dirty	sucio(a)	SSOOtheeyo(a)
cup	la taza	la TAtha	disc jockey	el disc jockey	el deessk DJOkey
cupboard	la alacena	la alaTHEna	district	el distrito	el deessTREEto
to cure	curar	kooRAR	to dive	tirarse	teeRARsse
curly	rizado(a)	rrreeTHAdo(a)	to divide	dividir	deebeeDEER
curly hair	el pelo rizado	el PElo rrreeTHAdo	divided by (math)	por	por
curtain	la cortina	la korTEEna	diving board	el trampolín	el trampoLEEN
customer (m)	el cliente	el kleeYENte	to do	hacer	aTHER
customer (f)	la clienta	la kleeYENta	to do back-stroke	hacer la braza de espalda	aTHER la BRAtha de essPALda
customs	la aduana	la adWAna	to do breast-stroke	hacer la braza de pecho	aTHER la BRAtha de PETsho
customs officer (m/f)	el aduanero	el adwaNEro	to do the dishes	fregar	freGAR
cut (wound)	la cortadura	la kortaDOOra	to do the gardening	cuidar el jardín	KWEEdar el charDEEN
			to do the shopping	hacer las compras	aTHER las KOMprass

D

			docks, quay	los muelles	loss mooWELyess
			doctor (m)	el médico	el MEdeeko
daisy	la margarita	la margaREEta	doctor (f)	la médica	la MEdeeka
to dance	bailar	baeeLAR	dog	el perro	el PErro
dance floor	la pista de baile	la PEESSta de BAeele	donkey	el burro	el BOOrro
			door	la puerta	la PWERta
dark (color)	oscuro(a)	ossKOOro(a)	front door	la puerta de entrada	la PWERta de enTRAda
dark (complexion)	moreno(a)	moREno(a)			
It is dark.	Es de noche.	ess de NOTshe	doorbell	el timbre	el TEEMbre
It is getting dark.	Oscurece.	osskooREthe	doormat	el felpudo	el felPOOdo
date	la fecha	la FETsha	double room	la habitación doble	la abeetaTHYON DOble
daughter	la hija	la EEcha			
only daughter	la hija única	la EEcha OOneeka	doughnut	el buñuelo	el boonYWElo
dawn	el amanecer	el amaneTHER	down	abajo	aBAcho
day, daytime, in the daytime	el día	el DEEya	downstairs	abajo	aBAcho
			to go downstairs	bajar	baCHAR
the day after tomorrow	pasado mañana	paSSAdo manYAna	dragonfly	la libélula	la leeBELoola
			to dream	soñar	ssonYAR
the day before yesterday	anteayer	anteaYER	dress	el vestido	el bessTEEdo
			to get dressed	vestirse	bessTEERsse
Dear…	Querido(a)…	keREEdo(a)	to drink	beber	beBER
Dear Sir/Madam	Muy señor mio:/ Estimada señora:	mooy ssenYOR MEEyo/ essteeMAda ssenYOra	to drive	conducir	kondooTHEER
			driver (m)	el conductor	el kondookTOR
			driver (f)	la conductora	la kondookTORa
			to drop	dejar caer	deCHAR kaER
death	la muerte	la mWERte	drums	los tambores	loss tamBOress
December	diciembre	deeTHYEMbre	to play the drums	tocar los tambores	toKAR loss tamBOress
deck	la cubierta	la kooBYERta			
deep	profundo(a)	proFOONdo(a)	to dry	secar	sseKAR
delicatessen	la fiambrería	la feeambreREEya	to dry your hair	secarse el pelo	sseKARsse el PElo
delicious	riquísimo(a)	rrreeKEEsseemo(a)	to dry yourself	secarse	sseKARsse
to deliver	entregar	entreGAR	duck	el pato	el PAto
democratic	democrático(a)	demoKRAteeko(a)	dull	apagado(a)	apaGAdo(a)
dentist (m/f)	el/la dentista	el/la denTEESSta	dungarees	el mono	el MOno
department (in shop)	el departamento	el departaMENto	duty-free shop	la tienda libre de impuestos	la TYENda LEEbre de eemPWESStos
department store	los grandes almacenes	loss GRANdess almaTHEness			
Departures	Salidas (f. pl)	ssaLEEdass			
desert	el desierto	el desseeYERto			
designer (m)	el diseñador	el deessenyaDOR	## E		
designer (f)	la diseñadora	la deessenyaDORa			
dessert, pudding	el postre	el POSStre			
diary	la agenda	la aCHENda	eagle	el águila (f)	el Ageela
to die	morirse	moREERsse	ear	la oreja	la oREcha
different	diferente	deefeRENte	earrings	los pendientes	loss pendYENtess
difficult	difícil	deeFEEtheel	east	el este	el ESSte

Easter	Pascua	PASSkwa
easy	fácil	FAtheel
to eat	comer	koMER
to have eaten well	haber comido bien	aBER koMEEdo BYEN
egg	el huevo	el WEbo
eight	ocho	OTsho
8 in the morning, 8 a.m.	las ocho de la mañana	lass OTsho de la manYAna
8 in the evening, 8 p.m.	las ocho de la noche	lass OTsho de la NOTshe
eighteen	dieciocho	deeyetheeOTsho
eighty	ochenta	otSHENta
elastic	la cinta elástica	la THEENta eLASSteeka
elbow	el codo	el KOdo
election	la elección	la elekTHYON
electricity	la electricidad	la elektree-theeDATH
elephant	el elefante	el eleFANte
elevator	el ascensor	el assthenSSOR
eleven	once	ONthe
emergency	la urgencia	la oorCHENtheeya
emergency room	urgencias	oorCHENtheeyass
to employ someone	emplear a alguien	empleAR a algeeYEN
employee (m)	el empleado	el empleAdo
employee (f)	la empleada	la empleAda
empty	vacío(a)	baTHEEyo(a)
to empty	vaciar	batheeYAR
to get engaged	hacerse novios	aTHERsse NObeeyoss
engine	la máquina	la MAkeena
English (language or subject)	el inglés	el eenGLESS
to enjoy, to like	gustarle a uno	goossTARle a OOno
Enjoy your meal!	¡Que aproveche!	ke aproBETshe
to enjoy yourself	divertirse	deeberTEERsse
enormous	enorme	eNORme
entrance	la entrada	la enTRAda
no entry (road sign)	dirección prohibida	deerekTHYON proeeBEEda
envelope	el sobre	el SSObre
Equator	el ecuador	el ekwaDOR
eraser	la goma	la GOma
escalator	la escalera móvil	la eskaLEra MObeel
Europe	Europa	eooROpa
evening, afternoon	la tarde	la TARde
this evening	esta tarde	ESSta TARde
8 in the evening (or at night)	las ocho de la noche	lass OTsho de la NOTshe
exam	el examen	el ekSSAmen
to fail an exam	suspender	ssoosspenDER
to pass an exam	aprobar	aproBAr
to take an exam	examinarse	ekssameeNARsse
exchange rate	el tipo de cambio	el TEEpo de KAMbeeyo
to exercise	entrenarse	entreNARsse
exercise book	el cuaderno	el kwaDERno
exhibition	la exposición	la eksspossee-THYON
exit	la salida	la ssaLEEda
expensive	caro(a)	KAro(a)
It's expensive.	Es algo caro.	ess ALgo KAro
eye	el ojo	el Ocho

F

fabric	la tela	la TEla
face	la cara	la KAra
factory	la fábrica	la FAbreeka
to fail an exam	suspender	ssoosspenDER
to faint	desmayarse	dezmaYARsse
fair (complexion)	blanco(a)	BLANGko(a)
to fall asleep	dormirse	dorMEERsse
false	falso(a)	FALsso(a)
family	la familia	la faMEEleeya
famous	famoso(a)	faMOsso(a)
far	lejos	LEchoss
far away from	lejos de	LEchoss de
How far is...?	¿A qué distancia está...?	a ke deessTAN-theeya essTA
fare	el precio del viaje	el PREtheeyo del beeAche
farm	la granja	la GRANcha
farmer (m)	el granjero	el granCHEro
farmer (f), farmer's wife	la granjera	la granCHEra
farmhouse	la casería	la kasseREEya
farmyard	el patio de labranza	el PAteeyo de laBRANtha
fashionable	de moda	de MOda
fast	rápido(a)	RRApeedo(a)
Fasten your seatbelts.	¡Abrocharse el cinturón!	abroCHARssee el theentooRONN
fat	gordo(a)	GORdo(a)
father	el padre	el PAdre
feather	la pluma	la PLOOma
February	febrero	feBREro
to feed	dar de comer	dar de koMER
to feel better	sentirse mejor	ssenTEERsse meCHOR
to feel ill	sentirse malo(a)	ssenTEERsse MAlo(a)
ferry	el ferry	el FEre
to fetch	traer	traER
field	el campo	el KAMpo
fifteen	quince	KEENthe
the fifth (for dates only)	el cinco	el THEENGko
fifty	cincuenta	theeKWENta
to fill	llenar	lyeNAR
to fill up with gas	llenar de gasolina	lyeNAR de gassoLEEna
to have a filling	empastarse un diente	empassTARsse un deeYENte
film (at movies or for camera)	la película	la peLEEkoola
It's fine.	Hace bueno.	Athe BWEno
finger	el dedo	el DEdo
fire	el fuego	el FWEgo
fire engine	el coche de bomberos	el KOTshe de bomBEross
to fire someone	despedir a alguien	desspeDEER a ALgeeyen
fire station	el parque de bomberos	el PARke de bomBEros
fireman	el bombero	el bomBEro
fireplace	la chimenea	la tsheemeNEa
the first	el primero	el preeMEro
first class	primera clase	preeMEra KLAsse
first floor	primer piso	preeMER PEEsso
first name	el nombre de pila	el NOMbre de PEEla
fish	el pescado	el pesKAdo

fish market	la pescadería	la pesskadeREEya
to go fishing	ir de pesca	eer de PEsska
fishing boat	la barca de pesca	la BARka de PEsska
fishing rod	la caña	la KANya
to keep fit	mantenerse en forma	manteNERsse en FORma
five	cinco	THEENGko
five past 10	las diez y cinco	lass deeYETH ee THEENGko
flag	la bandera	la banDEra
flat tire	la rueda deshinchada	la RRWEda desseenTSHAda
flavor, taste	el sabor	el ssaBOR
to float	flotar	floTAR
flock	el rebaño	el rreBANyo
flood	la inundación	la eenoonda-THYONN
floor	el suelo	el ssooWElo
first floor	primer piso (m)	preeMER PEEsso
ground floor	piso bajo (m)	PEEsso BAcho
second floor	segundo piso (m)	sseGOONdo PEEsso
florist's	la floristería	la floreessteREEya
flour	la harina	la arEEna
flower	la flor	la flor
bunch of flowers	un manojo de flores	oon maNOcho de FLOress
flowerbed	el macizo	el maTHEEtho
fly	la mosca	la MOSSka
to fly	volar	boLAR
fog	la niebla	la NYEbla
It's foggy.	Hay niebla.	aee NYEbla
to follow	seguir	sseGEER
to be fond of	tenerle cariño a	teNERle kaREENyo
foot	el pie	el peeYE
forget-me-not	la nomeolvides	la nomeolBEEdes
fork (table)	el tenedor	el teneDOR
fork (for gardening)	la horquilla	la orKEELya
form	el formulario	el formooLAreeyo
forty	cuarenta	kwaRENta
forwards	hacia adelante	Atheeya adeLANte
foundation cream	la crema base	la KREma BAsse
four	cuatro	KWAtro
the fourth (for dates only)	el cuatro	el KWAtro
fourteen	catorce	kaTORthe
fox	el zorro	el THOrrro
fraction	la fracción	la frakTHYON
France	Francia	FRANtheeya
freckles	las pecas	lass PEkas
freight train	el tren de mercancías	el tren de merkanTHEEyass
French (language or subject)	el francés	el franTHESS
fresh	fresco(a)	FRESSko(a)
Friday	viernes	BYERness
fridge	la nevera	la neBEra
friend (m)	el amigo	el aMEEgo
friend (f)	la amiga	la aMEEga
friendly	amistoso(a)	ameessTOsso(a)
frightened	asustado(a)	assoossTAdo(a)
frog	la rana	la RRAna
front door	la puerta de entrada	la PWERta de enTRAda
frost	la escarcha	la essKARTsha
to frown	fruncir el ceño	froonTHEER el THENyo
frozen food	los congelados	loss koncheLAdoss

to be frozen	estar helado(a)	essTAR eLAdo(a)
fruit	la fruta	la FROOta
fruit juice	el jugo de frutas	el CHOOgo de FROOtas
full	lleno(a)	LYEno(a)
to be fully booked	estar completo	essTAR komPLEto
to have fun	divertirse	deeberTEERsse
funeral	el entierro	el enteeYErrro
funny	gracioso(a)	gratheeOsso(a)
fur	el pelo	el PElo
furniture	los muebles	loss MWEbless
future	el futuro	el fooTOOro
in the future	en el futuro	en el fooTOOro

G

galaxy	la galaxia	la gaLAKsseeya
art gallery	la galería de arte	la galeREEya de ARte
game	los juegos	loss chooWEgoss
gangway	la pasarela	la passaRELa
garage	el garaje	el gaRAche
garbage collector	el basurero	el bassooREro
garden	el jardín	el charDEEN
garden shed	la caseta de jardín	la kaSSEta de charDEEN
gardener (m)	el jardinero	el chardeeNEro
to do the gardening	cuidar el jardín	KWEEdar el charDEEN
garlic	el ajo	el Acho
gas	el gas	el gass
gas	la gasolina	la gassoLEEna
gas station	la gasolinera	la gassoleeNEra
to fill up with gas	llenar de gasolina	lyeNAR de gassoLEEna
gate	la puerta	la PWERta
to gather speed	acelerar	atheleRAR
generous	generoso(a)	cheneROsso(a)
geography	la geografía	cheograFEEya
geranium	el geraneo	el cheRAneo
German (language or subject)	el alemán	el aleMAN
Germany	Alemana	aleMAna
to get dressed	vestirse	bessTEERsse
to get engaged	hacerse novios	aTHERsse NObeeyos
to get married	casarse	kaSSARsse
to get off (a bus or train)	bajarse	baCHARsse
to get on	subirse	sooBEERsse
to get undressed	quitarse la ropa	keeTARsse la RROpa
to get up	levantarse	lebanTARsse
giraffe	la jirafa	la cheeRAfa
girl	la niña	la NEENya
to give	dar	dar
to give (a present)	regalar	rrregaLAR
glass	el vaso	el BAsso
glasses, spectacles	las gafas	lass GAfass
sunglasses	las gafas de sol	lass GAfass de ssol
to wear glasses	llevar gafas	lyeBAR GAfass
gloves	los guantes	loss GWANtes
to go	ir	eer
to go to bed	acostarse	akossTARsse
to go to the movies	ir al cine	eer al THEEne
to go downstairs	bajar	baCHAR

English	Spanish	Pronunciation
to go fishing	ir de pesca	eer de PESSka
to go mountaineering	hacer el alpinismo	aTHER el alpeeNEEZmo
to go upstairs	subir	ssooBEER
to go on vacation	ir de vacaciones	eer de bakaTHYOness
to go for a walk	dar un paseo	dar un paSSEyo
to go window-shopping	ir de escaparates	eer de esskapaRAtess
to go to work	ir a trabajar	eer a trabaCHAR
goal	el gol	el gol
goalkeeper	el portero	el porTEro
goat	la cabra	la KAbra
gold	el oro	el Oro
made of gold	de oro	de Oro
goldfish	el pez de colores	el peth de koLOres
golf club	el palo de golf	el PAlo de golf
to play golf	jugar al golf	chooGAR al golf
good	bueno(a)	booWEno(a)
Good luck!	¡Buena suerte!	BWEna SSWERte
Good-morning	¡Buenos días!	BWEnoss DEEyass
It's good value.	No es caro.	no ess KAro
It tastes good.	Está muy rico.	essTA mooy RRREEko
Goodbye	¡Adiós!	adeeOSS
Good-night, See you tomorrow	¡Hasta mañana!	ASSta manYAna
goose	el ganso	el GANsso
gorilla	el gorila	el goREEla
government	el gobierno	el gobeeERno
grammar	la gramática	la graMAteeka
granddaughter	la nieta	la neeYEta
grandfather	el abuelo	el abooWElo
grandmother	la abuela	la abooWEla
grandson	el nieto	el neeEto
grape	la uva	la OOba
grass	la hierba	la YERba
Great Britain	Gran Bretaña	GRAN breTANya
green	verde	BERde
greenhouse	el invernadero	el eenbernaDEro
grey	gris	greess
grocery shop	(la tienda de) ultramarinos	(la TYENda de) ooltramaREEnoss
ground floor	piso bajo (m)	PEEsso BAcho
to growl	gruñir	grooNEER
guard	el interventor	el eenterbenTOR
guest (m)	el invitado	el eenbeeTAdo
guest house, boarding house	la pensión	la penseeYONN
guinea pig	el conejillo de Indias	el koneCHEELlyo de EEndeeyas
guitar	la guitarra	la geeTArrra
to play the guitar	tocar la guitarra	toKAR la geeTArrra
gymnastics	la gimnasia	la cheemNAsseeya

H

English	Spanish	Pronunciation
hail	el granizo	el graNEEtho
to hail a taxi	parar un taxi	paRAR oon TAKsee
hair	el pelo	el PELo
to have (...) color hair	tener el pelo...	teNER el PELo
hairdresser (m)	el peluquero	el pelooKEro
hairdresser (f)	la peluquera	la pelooKEra
hairdresser's	la peluquería	la pelookeREEya
hairdrier	la secadora eléctrica	la ssekaDOra eLEKtreeka

English	Spanish	Pronunciation
hake	la merluza	la merLOOtha
a half	medio	MEdeeyo
half a kilo	medio kilo	MEdyo KEElo
half a liter	medio litro	MEdyo LEEtro
half past 10	las diez y media	lass DYETH ee MEdeeya
half slip	las enaguas	lass eNAgwass
ham	el jamón	el chaMONN
hammer	el martillo	el marTEELlyo
hamster	el hámster	el AMster
hand	la mano	la MAno
handbag	el bolso	el BOLsso
hand luggage	el equipaje de mano	el ekeePAche de MAno
handsome	guapo(a)	GWApo(a)
to hang on to	colgarse a	kolGARsse a
to hang up (telephone)	colgar	kolGAR
happy	feliz	feLEETH
to be happy	ser feliz	sser feLEETH
Happy New Year	¡Feliz Año!	feLEETH ANyo
hard	duro(a)	DOOro(a)
hard-working	trabajador(a)	trabachaDOR(a)
to harvest	cosechar	kosseTSHAR
hat	el sombrero	el ssombRERo
Have you any small change?	¿Tiene cambio?	TYEne KAMbyo
to have	tener	teNER
to have a bath	bañarse	banYARsse
to have a breakdown (vehicle)	tener una avería	teNER oona abeREEya
to have a cold	tener un resfriado	teNER oon rrressfreeAdo
to have (...) color hair	tener el pelo...	teNER el PElo
to have a filling	empastarse un diente	empassTARsse oon DYENte
to have a flat tire	tener una rueda deshinchada	teNER oona RWEda desseenTSHAda
to have fun	divertirse	deberTEERsse
to have a shower	ducharse	dooTSHARsse
to have stomach ache	tener dolor de estómago	teNER doLOR de essTOmago
to have a temperature	tener fiebre	teNER FYEbre
to have toothache	tener dolor de muelas	teNER doLOR de MWElass
Having a lovely time.	Pasándolo muy bien.	paSSANdolo MOOY BYEN
hay	el heno	el Eno
haystack	el almiar	el alMEEar
head	la cabeza	la kaBEtha
to have a headache	tener dolor de cabeza	teNER doLOR de kaBEtha
headband	la sudadera	la ssoodaDEra
headlight	el faro	el FAro
headlines	los titulares	loss teetooLAress
headphones	los auriculares	loss aureekooLAress
healthy	sano(a)	SSAno(a)
heavy	pesado(a)	peSSAdo(a)
to be heavy	ser pesado(a)	sser peSSAdo(a)
hedgehog	el erizo	el eREEtho
heel	el talón	el taLONN
height	la altura	la alTOOra
Hello	¡Hola!	Ola
Hello (on telephone)	¡Dígame!	DEEgame

to help	ayudar	ayooDAR
Help yourself!	¡Sírvete!	SEERbete
Can I help you?	¿Qué desea?	ke deSSEa
hen	la gallina	la galYEEna
henhouse	el gallinero	el galyeeNEro
hero	el héroe	el Eroe
heroine	la heroína	la eroEEna
to hide	esconderse	esskonDERsse
hill	el cerro	el THErrno
hippopotamus	el hipopótamo	el eepoPOtamo
His name is...	El se llama...	el sse LYAma
history	la historia	la eessTOreeya
hold (ship's)	la bodega	la boDEga
to hold	tener	teNER
honey	la miel	la MYEL
honeymoon	el viaje de novios	el beeYAche de NObeeyoss
hood (of car)	el capó	el kaPO
hook (for fishing)	el anzuelo	el enTHWElo
horn	la bocina	la boTHEEna
horse	el caballo	el kaBALyo
horse racing	las carreras de caballos	lass kaRRRErass de kaBALyoss
hospital	el hospital	el osspeeTAL
hot	caliente	kaleeYENte
hot water	el agua (f) caliente	el Agwa kaleeYENte
I'm hot.	Tengo calor.	TENGgo kaLOR
hotel	el hotel	el oTEL
to stay in a hotel	quedar en un hotel	keDAR en oon oTEL
hour	la hora	la Ora
house	la casa	la KAssa
How are you?	¿Qué tal?	ke TAL
How far is...?	¿A qué distancia está...?	a ke deessTANtheya essTA
how much...?	cuánto...?	KWANto
How much do I owe you?	¿Cuánto es todo?	KWANto ess TOdo
How much is...?	¿Cuánto cuesta...?	KWANto KWESSta
How old are you?	¿Cuántos años tienes?	KWANtoss ANyos TYEness
hump	la giba	la CHEEba
a hundred	ciento	THYENto
to be hungry	tener hambre	teNER AMbre
to hurry	darse prisa	DARsse PREEssa
husband	el marido	el maREEdo

I

I agree	De acuerdo.	de aKWERdo
I am sending (...) separately.	Te mando por separado...	te MANdo por ssepaRAdo
I enclose...	Adjunto...	adCHOONto
I'll call you back.	Te llamo más tarde.	te LYAmo mass TARde
I would like...	Querría...	keRRREEya
I'm nineteen.	Tengo diecinueve años.	TENGgo dyetheeNWEbe ANyoss
ice-cream	el helado	el eLAdo
icicle	el carámbano	el kaRAMbano
ill	malo(a)	MAlo(a)
to feel ill	sentirse malo(a)	ssenTEERsse MAlo(a)
important	importante	eemporTANte
in (for sports)	dentro	DENtro
in	en	en

in focus	en foco	en FOko
in front of	delante de	deLANte de
in the future	en el futuro	en el fooTOOro
India	la India	la EEndeeya
indicator	el indicador	el eendeekaDOR
ingredient	el ingrediente	el eengreDYENte
injection	la inyección	la eenyekTHYON
instrument	el instrumento	el eensstrooMENto
inter-city train	el tren TALGO	el tren TALgo
interesting	interesante	eentereSSANte
to interview	entrevistar	entrebeessTAR
into	dentro	DENtro
to introduce	presentar	pressenTAR
to invite	invitar	eenbeeTAR
to iron	planchar	planISHAR
Is service included?	¿Está incluido el servicio?	essTA eenklooEEdo el sserBEEtheeyo
It costs...	Cuesta...	KWESSTA
It is getting light.	Amanece.	amanNEthe
It is light.	Es de día.	ess de DEEya
It is 1 o'clock.	Es la una.	ess la OOna
It is 3 o'clock.	Son las tres.	sson lass TRESS
It's...(on phone)	Soy...	ssoy
It's cold.	Hace frío.	Athe FREEyo
It's expensive.	Es algo caro.	ess ALgo KAro
It's fine.	Hace bueno.	Athe BWEno
It's foggy.	Hay niebla.	Ay NYEbla
It's good value.	No es caro.	no ess KAro
It's raining.	Llueve.	lyooEbe
It's ready. (meal)	Ya está.	ya essTA
It's snowing.	Nieva.	NYEba
It's windy.	Hace viento.	Athe BYENto
It was lovely to hear from you.	Me encantó tener noticias tuyas.	me enkanTO teNER noTEEtheeyass TOOyas
Italy	Italia	eeTAleeya

J

jacket	la chaqueta	la tshaKEta
jam	la mermelada	la mermeLAda
January	enero	eNEro
Japan	el Japón	el chaPONN
jeans	los vaqueros	los baKEross
jewelry	las joyas	lass CHOyass
job, profession	la profesión	la profeSYON
to jog	hacer fúting	aTHER FOOteen
to join	asociarse	assotheeARsse
journalist (m/f)	el/la periodista	el/la pereeoDEESSta
judge	el juez	el CHWEth
juice	el jugo	el CHOOgo
fruit juice	el jugo de frutas	el CHOOgo de FROOtass
July	julio	CHOOleeyo
June	junio	CHOOneeyo
jungle	la selva	la SSELba

K

kangaroo	el canguro	el kanGOOro
to keep an eye on	vigilar	beegeeLAR
to keep fit	mantenerse en forma	manteNERsse en FORma
kennel	la perrera	la peRRRERa

keyboard	el teclado	el teKLAdo
kilo	el kilo	el KEElo
A kilo of...	Un kilo de...	oon KEElo de
Half a kilo of...	Medio kilo de...	MEdyo KEElo de
to kiss	dar un beso	dar oon BEsso
kitchen	la cocina	la koTHEEna
kitten	el gatito	el gaTEEto
knee	la rodilla	la rrroDEELya
to kneel down	arrodillarse	arrrodeelYARsse
to be kneeling	estar de rodillas	essTAR de rrroDEELyass
knife	el cuchillo	el kootSHEELyo
to knit	hacer punto	aTHER POONto
knitting needles	las agujas	lass AGOOchass
to knock over	volcar	bolKAR

L

label	la etiqueta	la eteeKEta
ladder	la escalera	la esskaLEra
lake	el lago	el LAgo
lamb	el cordero	el korDEro
lamp	la lámpara	la LAMpara
to land	aterrizar	aterrreeTHAR
landlady	la patrona	la paTROna
landlord	el patrón	el paTRONN
landscape	el paisaje	el paeeSSAche
large	grande	GRANde
last	último(a)	OOlteemo(a)
to be late	llevar retraso	lyeBAR rrreTRAsso
to arrive late	llegar tarde	lyeGAR TARde
Latin America	América Latina	aMEreeka laTEEna
to laugh	reír	rrreEEr
to burst out laughing	echarse a reír	eTSHARsse a rrreEER
lawn	el césped	el THESSpeth
lawnmower	el cortacésped	el kortaTHESSpeth
lawyer (m)	el abogado	el aboGAdo
lawyer (f)	la abogada	la aboGAda
to lay eggs	poner huevos	poNER WEboss
lazy	perezoso(a)	pereTHOsso(a)
leader (m)	el jefe	el CHEfe
leader (f)	la jefa	la CHEfa
leaf	la hoja	la Ocha
to lean on	apoyarse en	apoYARsse en
to learn	aprender	aPRENder
left luggage office	la consigna	la konSSEEGna
on the left	a la izquierda	a la eethKYERda
left, left side	el lado izquierdo	el LAdo eethKYERdo
left wing	de izquierdas	de eethKYERdass
leg	la pierna	la PYERna
leg of lamb	la pierna de cordero	la PYERna de korDEro
lemon	el limón	el leeMONN
length	el largo	el LARgo
lesson	la lección	la lekTHYON
letter	la carta	la KARta
letter of alphabet	la letra	la LEtra
liberal (politics)	de centro	de THENtro
library	la biblioteca	la beebleeooTEka
license plate	la matrícula	la maTREEKoola
to lie down	tumbarse	toomBARsse
life	la vida	la BEEda
lifeguard	el vigilante de playa	el beecheeLANte de PLAya
light (weight)	ligero(a)	leeCHEro(a)
to be light (weight)	ser ligero(a)	sser leeCHEro(a)

light	la luz	la LOOTH
It is light.	Es de día.	ess de DEEya
It is getting light.	Amanece.	amaNEthe
lightning	los relámpagos	loss rrreLAMpagoss
to line up	hacer cola	aTHER kola
liner	el trasatlántico	el trassadLANteeko
lion	el león	el leONN
lip	el labio	el LAbeeyo
lipstick	la barra de labios	la BArrra de LAbeeyos
list	la lista	la LEESSta
to make a list	hacer una lista	aTHER oona LEESSta
to listen	escuchar	esskooTSHAR
to listen to music	escuchar música	esskooTSHAR MOOsseeka
to listen to the radio	escuchar la radio	esskooTSHAR la RRRAdeeyo
liter	el litro	el LEEtro
half a liter	medio litro	MEDyo LEEtro
to live	vivir	beeBEER
to live in a house	vivir en una casa	beeBEER en oona KAssa
lively	animado(a)	aneeMAdo
living room	la sala de estar	la SSAla de essTAR
to load	cargar	karGAR
long	largo(a)	LARgo(a)
Look forward to seeing you soon.	Deseando verte pronto.	desseANdo BErte PRONto
to look at	mirar	meeRAR
to look for	buscar	boossKAR
loose	suelto(a)	SSWELto(a)
to lose	perder	perDER
loudspeaker	el altavoz	el altaBOTH
Love from... (end of letter)	Un abrazo de...	oon abRAtho de
to love	querer a	keRER a
lovely, beautiful	bonito(a)	boNEEto(a)
luck	la suerte	la SSWERte
Good luck	¡Buena suerte!	BWEna SSWERte
luggage cart	la carretilla	la karrreTEELya
luggage-rack	la rejilla	la rrreCHEELya
lullaby	la canción de cuna	la kanTHYONN de KOOna
lunch	el almuerzo	el alMWERtho
lunch hour	la hora de comer	la Ora de koMER
to be lying down	estar echado(a)	essTAR eTSHAdo(a)

M

made of metal	de metal	de meTAL
made of plastic	de plástico	de PLASSteeko
magazine	la revista	la rrreBEESSta
mail	el correo	el koRREo
to mail	echar al correo	etSHAR al koRRREo
mailbox	el buzón	el booTHONN
airmail	por avión	por abYONN
main course	el primer plato	el preeMER PLAto
main road	la carretera	la karrreTEra
to make a list	hacer una lista	aTHER oona LEESSta
to make a telephone call	hacer una llamada	aTHER oona lyaMAda
to make, to manufacture	hacer	aTHER
to put on make-up	maquillarse	makeelYARsse
man	el hombre	el OMbre

map	el mapa	el MApa
March	marzo	MARtho
margarine	la margarina	la margaREEna
market	el mercado	el merKAdo
market stall	el puesto	el PWESSto
marriage	el casamiento	el kassaMYENto
to get married	casarse	kaSSARsse
mascara	el rímel	el RRREEmel
math	las matemáticas	lass mateMAteekass
May	mayo	MAyo
meadow	el prado	el PRAdo
measure	medir	meDFFR
meat	la carne	la KARne
mechanic (m)	el mecánico	el meKAneeko
the media	los medios de comunicación	loss MEDeeyoss de komooneeka-THYONN
medium (clothes size)	mediano	medYAno
to meet	encontrarse con	enkonTRARsse kon
melon	el melón	el meLONN
member (m/f)	el miembro	el MYEMbro
member of parliament (m)	el diputado	el deepooTAdo
member of parliament (f)	la diputada	la deepooTAda
to mend	reparar	rrrePArar
to mend (clothing)	zurcir	thoorTHEER
menu	el menú	el meNOO
merry-go-round	el tiovivo	el teeyoBEEbo
metal	el metal	el meTAL
made of metal	de metal	de meTAL
meter	el metro	el MEtro
to mew	maullar	maoolYAR
midday	mediodía	medyoDEEya
midnight	medianoche	medyaNOTshe
milk	la leche	la LEtshe
to milk	ordeñar	ordenYAR
a million	un millón	oon meelYONN
mineral water	el agua (f) mineral	el Agwa meeneRAL
minus, less	menos	MEnoss
minute	el minuto	el meeNOOto
mirror	el espejo	el essPEcho
miserable	triste	TRIste
to miss the train	perder el tren	perDER el TRENN
to mix	mezclar	methKLAR
model (m/f)	el/la modelo	el/la moDElo
mole	el topo	el TOpo
Monday	lunes(m)	LOOness
money	el dinero	el deeNEro
to change money	cambiar dinero	kambYAR deeNEro
to put money in the bank	meter dinero en el banco	meTER deeNEro en el BANGko
to take money out	sacar dinero del banco	saKAR deeNEro del BANGko
monkey	el mono	el MOno
month	el mes	el mess
moon	la luna	la LOOna
moped	el ciclomotor	el theeklomoTOR
morning	la mañana	la manYAna
8 in the morning, 8 a.m.	las ocho de la mañana	lass OTsho de la manYAna
this morning	esta mañana	essta manYAna
mosquito	el mosquito	el mossKEEto
mother	la madre	la MAdre
motor racing	las carreras de coches	lass kaRRERass de KOTshess
motorbike	la motocicleta	la mototheeKLEta

motorway	la autopista	la aootoPEESSta
mountain	la montaña	la monTANya
mountaineering	el alpinismo	el alpeeNEESSmo
to go mountaineering	hacer el alpinismo	aTHER el alpeeNEESSmo
mouse	el ratón	el rrraTONN
moustache	el bigote	el beeGOte
to have a moustache	tener bigote	teNER beeGOte
mouth	la boca	la BOka
to move in	venirse a vivir	beNEERse a beeBEER
to move out	mudarse	mooDARsse
movie(s)	el cine	el THEEne
to go to the movies	ir al cine	eir al THEEne
to mow the lawn	cortar el césped	korTAR el THESSpeth
to multiply	multiplicar	moolteepleeKAR
music	la música	la MOOsseeka
classical music	la música clásica	la MOOsseeka KLAsseeka
pop music	la música pop	la MOOsseeka pop
musician (m/f)	el/la músico	el/la MOOsseeko
mustard	la mostaza	la mossTAtha
My name is...	Me llamo...	me lYAmo

N

naked	desnudo(a)	dezNOOdo(a)
name	el nombre	el NOMbre
first name	el nombre de pila	el NOMbre de PEEla
surname	el apellido	el apelYEEdo
His name is...	El se llama...	el sse LYAma
My name is...	Me llamo...	me LYAmo
What's your name?	¿Cómo te llamas?	KOmo te lYAmass
napkin	la servilleta	la sserbeelYFta
narrow	estrecho(a)	essTRETsho(a)
naughty	travieso(a)	traBYEsso(a)
navy blue	azul marino	aTHOOL maREEno
near	cerca de	THERka de
neck	el cuello	el KWELyo
necklace	el collar	el kolYAR
needle	la aguja	la aGOOcha
needlecraft shop, haberdasher's	la mercería	la mertheREEya
neighbor (m)	el vecino	el beTHEEno
neighbor (f)	la vecina	la beTHEEna
nephew	el sobrino	el ssoBREEno
nest	el nido	el NEEdo
net	la red	la rreth
Netherlands	Holanda	oLANda
new	nuevo(a)	NWEbo(a)
New Year's Day	el día de Año Nuevo	el DEEya de ANyo NWEbo
New Year's Eve	Nochevieja	notsheBYEcha
Happy New Year	¡Feliz Año!	feLEETh ANyo
New Zealand	Nueva Zelanda	NWEba theLANda
news	las noticias	lass noTEEtheeyas
newspaper	el periódico	el pereeOdeeko
newspaper stand	el quiosco de periódicos	el keeOSSko de pereeOdeekoss
next	próximo(a)	PROKsseemo
next, following	siguiente	sseeGYEnte
the next day	al día siguiente	al DEEya seeGYENte
next Monday	el lunes próximo	el LOOness PROKsseemo

next week	la semana próxima	la sseMAna PROKsseema
niece	la sobrina	la soBREEna
night	la noche	la NOTshe
nightclub	la sala de fiestas	la SSAla de FYESStass
to go to a nightclub	ir a una sala de fiestas	eer a oona SSAla de FYESStas
nightgown	el camisón	el kameeSSON
nine	nueve	NWEbe
911 call	la llamada de urgencia	la lyaMAda de oorCHENtheeya
nineteen	diecinueve	deeyetheeNWEbe
ninety	noventa	noBENta
no	no	no
no entry (road sign)	dirección prohibida	deerekTHYON proeeBEEda
no parking	¡Prohibido el estacionamiento!	proeeBEEdo el esstathyona-MYENto
no smoking	Prohibido fumar	proeeBEEdo fooMAR
noisy	ruidoso(a)	rrrooeeDOsso(a)
north	el norte	el NORte
North Pole	el polo norte	el POlo NORte
nose	la nariz	la naREETH
nothing	nada	NAda
nothing to declare	nada que declarar	NAda ke deklaRAR
novel	la novela	la NOBela
November	noviembre	noBYEMbre
now, nowadays	ahora	aOra
nurse (m)	el enfermero	el enferMEro
nurse (f)	la enfermera	la enferMEra

O

oak tree	el roble	el RRROble
oar	el remo	el REmo
obedient	obediente	obeDYENte
It is one o'clock.	Es la una.	ess la OOna
It is 3 o'clock.	Son las tres.	sson lass TRESS
October	octubre	okTOObre
office	la oficina	la ofeeTHEEna
offices, office block	el bloque de oficinas	el BLOke de ofeeTHEEnass
oil (engine/food)	el aceite	el aTHEYte
old	viejo(a)	BYEcho(a)
older, elderly	mayor	maYOR
older than	mayor que	maYOR ke
old-fashioned	anticuado(a)	anteeKWAdo
old age	la vejez	la beCHETH
on	sobre	SSObre
one	uno(a)	OOno(a)
onion	la cebolla	la theBOLya
open	abierto(a)	aBYERto(a)
to open	abrir	aBREER
to open a letter	abrir una carta	aBREER oona KARta
to open the curtains	descorrer las cortinas	desskoRRRER las korTEEnass
opera	la ópera	la Opera
operating theatre	el quirófano	el keeROfano
operation	la intervención cirúrgica	la eenterbenTHYON theeROORcheeka
opposite	frente a	FRENte a
orange (color)	anaranjado	anaranCHAdo
orange (fruit)	la naranja	la naRANcha

orchard	el huerto	el WERto
orchestra	la orquesta	la orKESSta
to order, to ask for	pedir	peDEER
ostrich	el avestruz	el abeSSTROOTH
out (for sports)	fuera	FWEra
out, out of	fuera	FWEra
out of focus	fuera de foco	FWEra de FOko
oven	el horno	el ORno
over	por encima de	por enTHEEma de
overtime	horas (f.pl) extraordinarias	Orass esstraordee-NAreeyass
owl	el buho	el BOOo

P

Pacific Ocean	el Pacífico	el paTHEEfeeko
to pack	hacer la maleta	aTHER la maLEta
package	el paquete	el paKEte
packet	el paquete	el paKEte
to paddle	chapotear	tshapoteAR
paint	la pintura	la peenTOOra
to paint	pintar	peenTAR
painter (m)	el pintor	el peenTOR
painter (f)	la pintora	la peenTOra
painting	el cuadro	el KWAdro
pajamas	el pijama	el peeCHAma
pale	claro(a)	KLAro(a)
panties	las bragas	lass BRAgass
paper	el papel	el paPEL
paper money	el billete	el beelYEte
paperback	la edicíon de bolsillo	la edeeTHYONN de bolSEELyo
parents	los padres	loss PAdress
park	el parque	el PARke
park keeper	el vigilante (de parque)	el beecheeLANte (de PARke)
to park	aparcar	aparKAR
no parking	¡Prohibido el estacionamiento!	proeeBEEdo el essta-theeonaMYENto
parliament	el parlamento	el parlaMENto
party (celebration)	la fiesta	la FYEssta
party (political)	el partido	el parTEEdo
to pass (in car)	adelantar	adelanTAR
to pass an exam	aprobar	aproBAR
passenger (m)	el pasajero	el passaCHEro
passenger (f)	la pasajera	la passaCHEra
passport	el pasaporte	el passaPORte
past	el pasado	el paSSAdo
pasta	los fideos	loss feeDEyoss
pastry, cake	el pastel	el passTEL
path, small path	el sendero	el ssenDEro
path, country lane	el camino	el kaMEEno
patient (m/f)	el/la paciente	el/la paTHYENte
pattern	el patrón	el paTRONN
pavement	la acera	la aTHEra
paw	la pata	la PAta
PE	la gimnasia	la cheemNAsseeya
pea	el guisante	el geeSSANte
peaceful	tranquilo(a)	tranKEElo(a)
peach	el melocotón	el melokoTONN
pear	la pera	la PEra
pedestrian	el peatón	el peaTONN
pedestrian crossing	el cruce de peatones	el KROOthe de peaTOness
pen	la pluma	la PLOOma
ball-point pen	el bolígrafo	el boLEEgrafo
pencil	el lápiz	el LApeeth

120

English	Spanish	Pronunciation
pencil case	la caja de lápices	la KAcha de LApeethess
penguin	el pingüino	el peenGWEEno
pepper	la pimienta	la peeMYEnta
to perch	posarse	poSSARsse
to perform, to appear on stage	actuar	aktooAR
perfume	el perfume	el perFOOme
period	el punto	el POONto
petticoat, slip	la combinación	la kombeena-THYONN
pharmacy	la farmacia	la farMAtheeya
photograph	la foto	la FOto
to take a photograph	tomar una foto	toMAR oona FOto
photographer (m)	el fotógrafo	el foTOgrafo
photographer (f)	la fotógrafa	la foTOgrafa
photography	la fotografía	la fotograFEEya
physics	la física	la FEEsseeka
piano	el piano	el PYAno
to play the piano	tocar el piano	toKAR el PYAno
to pick	coger	koCHER
to pick flowers	coger flores	koCHER FLOress
to pick up	recoger	rrrekoCHER
to pick up the receiver	descolgar	desskolGAR
picnic, afternoon tea	la merienda	la mereeYENda
pig	el cerdo	el THERdo
pigeon	la paloma	la paLOma
pill	la pastilla	la passTEELya
pillow	la almohada	la almoAda
pilot	el piloto	el peeLOto
pin	el alfiler	el alfeeLER
pine tree	el pino	el PEEno
pink	rosado(a)	rrroSSAdo(a)
to pitch a tent	montar la tienda de campaña	monTAR la TYENda de kamPANya
pitcher	el jarro	el cHArrro
planet	el planeta	el plaNEta
plate	el plato	el PLAto
to plant	plantar	planTAR
plastic	el plástico	PLASSteeko
made of plastic	de plástico	de PLASSteeko
platform	el andén	el anDENN
platform ticket	el billete de andén	el beelYEte de anDENN
play (theatre)	la obra de teatro	la Obra de teAtro
to play (an instrument)	tocar	toKAR
to play (games)	jugar	chooGAR
to play cards	jugar a las cartas	chooGAR a lass KARtass
to play checkers	jugar a las damas	chooGAR a lass DAmass
to play chess	jugar al ajedrez	chooGAR al acheDRETH
to play golf	jugar al golf	chooGAR al GOLF
to play soccer	jugar al fútbol	chooGAR al FOODbol
to play squash	jugar al scuach	chooGAR al essKWAch
to play tennis	jugar al tenis	chooGAR al TEneess
playful	juguetón	choogeTONN
playground	el patio de juego	el PAteeyo de CHWEgo
pleased with	contento(a) con	konTENto(a) kon
to plow	arar	aRAR
plug (electric)	el enchufe	el enTSHOOfe
plug (for bath)	el tapón de baño	el taPONN de BANyo
plum	la ciruela	la theerooWEla
plumber	el fontanero	el fontaNEro
plus	más	mass
pocket	el bolsillo	el bolSSEELyo
poetry	la poesía	la poeSSEEya
polar bear	el oso blanco	el Osso BLANGko
police	la policía	la poleeTHEEya
police car	el coche de policía	el KOTshe de poleeTHEEya
police station	la comisaría	la komeessaREEya
policeman	el guardia	el GWARdeeya
policewoman	la guardia	la GWARdceya
polite	educado(a)/bien educado(a)	edooKAdo/byen edooKAdo(a)
politics	la política	la poLEEteeka
pond	el estanque	el essTANke
poppy	la amapola	la amaPOla
popular	popular	popuLAR
pork chop	la chuleta de cerdo	la TSHOOleta de THERdo
port	el puerto	el PWEKto
porter	el mozo	el MOtho
porthole	la portilla	la porTEELya
post office	correos (m. pl)	koRRREoss
postcard	la tarjeta postal	la tarCHEta possTAL
postman	el cartero	el karTEro
potato	la patata	la paTAta
to pour	verter	berTHER
powerboat	la lancha motora	la LANtsha moTOra
prescription	la receta	la rreTHEta
present (gift)	el regalo	el rrreGAlo
present (now)	el presente	el preSSENte
president	el presidente	el presseeDENte
president (f)	la presidenta	la presseeDENta
pretty	bonito(a)	boNEEto(a)
price	el precio	el PREtheeyo
prime minister (m)	el primer ministro	el preeMER meeNEESStro
prime minister (f)	la primera ministra	la preeMEra meeNEESStra
printed	estampado(a)	esstamPAdo(a)
program	el programa	el proGRAma
pudding	el postre	el POSStre
puddle	el charco	el TSHARko
to take someone's pulse	tomar el pulso	toMAR el POOLsso
to pull	tirar	teeRAR
pupil (m)	el alumno	el aLOOMno
pupil (f)	la alumna	la aLOOMna
puppy	el cachorro	el katSHOrrro
purple	morado(a)	moRAdo(a)
to purr	ronronear	rrronroneAR
purse	el monedero	el moneDEro
to push	empujar	empooCHAR
to put	meter	meTER
to put down	depositar	deposeeTAR
to put money in the bank	meter dinero en el banco	meTER deeNEro en el BANGko

Q

a quarter	un cuarto	oon KWARto
a quarter past 10	las diez y cuarto	lass DYETH ee KWARto
a quarter to 10	las diez menos cuarto	la DYETH MEnoss KWARto
to ask a question	preguntar	pregoonTAR
quiet, silent	callado(a)	kalYAdo(a)
quilt	el duvé	el dooBE

R

rabbit	el conejo	el koNEcho
races, racing	las carreras	las kaRRRErass
racket	la raqueta	la rrraKEta
radiator	el radiador	el rrradeeyaDOR
radio	la radio	la RRRAdeeyo
rail car	el vagón	el baGONN
railway	el ferrocarril	el ferrrokaRRREEL
rain	la lluvia	la lYOObeeya
rainbow	el arcoiris	el arkoEErees
raincoat	el impermeable	el eempermeAble
raindrop	la gota de lluvia	la GOta de lYOObeeya
to rain	llover	lyoBER
It's raining.	Llueve.	lWEbe
rake	el rastrillo	el rrrassTREELyo
raspberry	la frambuesa	la framBWEssa
raw	crudo(a)	KROOdo(a)
razor	la maquinilla de afeitar	la makeeNEELya de afeyTAR
to read	leer	leER
to read a book	leer un libro	leER oon LEEbro
to read a story	leer un cuento	leER oon KWENto
It's ready.	Ya está.	ya essTA
receipt	el recibo	el rrreTHEEbo
to receive	recibir	rrretheeBEER
receiver	el auricular	el aooreekooLAR
reception	la recepción	la rrrethep-THYONN
recipe	la receta	la rrreTHEta
record	el disco	el DEESSko
record player	el tocadiscos	el tokaDEESSkoss
record shop	la tienda de discos	la TYENda de DEESSkoss
rectangle	el rectángulo	el rrrekTANgoolo
red	rojo(a)	RRRocho(a)
red hair	el pelo rojo	el PElo RRROocho
reed	el junco	el CHOONko
referee	el árbitro	el ARbeetro
to be related	ser parientes	sser pareeYENtess
to reserve	reservar	rrresserBAR
to reserve a room	reservar una habitación	rrresserBAR OOna abeetaTHYONN
to reserve a seat	reservar un asiento	rrresserBAR oon aSSYENto
reserved seat	asiento reservado	aSSYENto rrresserBAdo
to rest	descansar	desskanSSAR
restaurant	el restorán	el rrresstoRAN
to retire	jubilarse	choobeeLARsse
by return mail	a vuelta de correo	a BWELta de koRREo
return ticket	el billete de ida y vuelta	el beelYEte de EEDa ee BWELta
rice	el arroz	el aRRROTH
to ride a bicycle	ir en bicicleta	eer en beetheeKLEta
on the right	a la derecha	a la deRETsha
right side	el lado derecho	el lado deRETsho
right wing	de derechas	de deRETshass
ring	la sortija	la ssorTEEcha
to ring	sonar	ssoNAR
to ring the bell	tocar el timbre	toKAR el TEEMbre
ripe	maduro(a)	maDOOro(a)
river	el río	el REEyo
road	la carretera	la karrreTEra
to roar	rugir	rrrooCHEER
robe	la bata	la BAta
rock pool	la charco de playa	la TSHarko de PLAya
roll	el panecillo	el paneTHEELyo
roof	el tejado	el teCHAdo
room	la habitación	la abeetaTHYONN
double room	la habitación doble	la abeetaTHYONN DOble
single room	la habitación individual	la abeetaTHYONN eendee-beedooAL
rooster	el gallo	el GALyo
rose	la rosa	la RRROssa
to row	remar	rrreMAR
rowing boat	la barca de remo	la BARka de RRREmo
to rub your eyes	frotarse los ojos	froTARsse loss Ochos
rubber boots	las botas de goma	lass botass de GOma
rucksack, backpack	la mochila	la motSHEEla
rude	mal educado(a)	mal edooKAdo(a)
ruler	la regla	la RRREgla
to run	correr	koRRRER
to run a bath	poner el bãno	poNER el BANyo
to run away	escapar	esskaPAR
running shoes	loz zapatos de corredor	loss thaPAtoss de korreDOR
runway	la pista de aterrizaje	la PEEsta de aterrreTHAche
Russia	Rusia	RRROOseeya

S

safety belt	el cinturón de seguridad	el theentooRONN de ssegooreeDATH
sailor	el marinero	el mareeNEro
salad	la ensalada	la enssaLAda
salami	el salchichón	el saltshee-TSHONN
sale (in shop)	saldos (m pl)	SSALdoss
sales representative (m/f)	el/la representante comercial	el/la rrrepressenTANte komerTHYAL
salt	la sal	la ssal
same	igual	eeGWAL
the same age	la misma edad	la MEEZma eDATH
sand	la arena	la aREna
sandals	las sandalias	lass ssanDAleeyass
sandcastle	el castillo de arena	el kassTEELyo de aREna
satchel	la cartera	la karTEra

122

English	Spanish	Pronunciation
Saturday	sábado (m)	SSAbado
saucepan	la cacerola	la katheROla
saucer	el platillo	el plaTEElyo
sausage	la salchicha	la ssalTSHEEtsha
sausage (spicy, cooked)	el chorizo	el tshoREEtho
saw	la sierra	la SSYErrra
to say	decir	deTHEER
scales	la báscula	la BASSkoola
Scandinavia	Escandinavia	esskandeeNAbeeya
scarecrow	el espantapájaros	el esspanta-PAchaross
scarf	la bufanda	la booFANda
scenery	el decorado de escena	el dekoRAdo de essTHEna
at school	en el colegio	en el koLEcheeyo
high school	el colegio	el koLEcheeyo
nursery school	el jardín infantil	el charDEEN eenfanTEEL
at nursery school	en el jardín infantil	en el charDEEN eenfanTEEL
primary school	la escuela primaria	la essKWEla preeMAreeya
scissors	las tijeras	lass teeCHErass
to score a goal	marcar un gol	marKAR oon gol
screwdriver	el atornillador	el atorneelyaDOR
sea	el mar	el mar
sea bream	el besugo	el beSSOOgo
seagull	la gaviota	la gabeeYOta
to be seasick	marearse	mareARsse
season	la estación	la esstaTHYONN
season ticket	el billete de abono	el beelYEte de aBOno
seasoning	el condimento/los condimentos	loss kondeeMENtoss
seat	el asiento	el aSSYENto
seat (at movies, theatre)	la butaca	la booTAka
reserved seat	asiento reservado	aSSYENto rrresserBAdo
seaweed	las algas marinas	lass ALgass maREEnas
second (unit of time)	el segundo	el sseGOONdo
second	segundo(a)	sseGOONdo(a)
the second (for dates only)	el dos	el doss
second class	segunda clase	sseGOONda KLAsse
second floor	segundo piso (m)	sseGOONdo PEEsso
secretary (m)	el secretario	el ssekreTAreeyo
secretary	la secretaria	la ssekreTAreeya
See you later.	¡Hasta pronto!	ASSta PRONto
seeds	las semillas	lass sseMEELyass
to sell	vender	benDER
to send	mandar	manDAR
am sending (...) separately.	Te mando por separado...	te MANdo por ssepaRAdo
to send a postcard	mandar una postal	manDAR OOna possTAL
to send a telegram	mandar un telegrama	manDAR oon teleGRAma
sentence	la frase	la FRAsse
September	setiembre	sseTYEMbre
to serve (a meal)	servir	sserBEER
to serve (tennis)	servir	sserBEER
service	el servicio	el sserBEEtheyyo
Is service included?	¿Está incluido el servicio?	essTA eenklooEEdo el sserBEEtheeyo
Service is not included.	El servicio no está incluido.	el sserBEEtheeyo no essTA eenklooEEdo
to set the table	poner la mesa	poNER le MEssa
seven	siete	ssYEte
seventeen	diecisiete	deeyetheeSYEte
seventy	setenta	sseTENta
to sew	coser	koSSER
shade	la sombra	la SSOMbra
to shake	sacudir	ssakooDEER
to shake hands	dar la mano	dar la MAno
shallow	poco profundo(a)	POko pruFOONdo(a)
shampoo	el champú	el tshamPOO
shape	la forma	la FORma
to shave	afeitarse	afeyTARsse
electric shaver	la afeitadora eléctrica	la afeytaDOra eLEKtreeka
shaving foam	la espuma de afeitar	la esspooma de afeyTAR
sheep	la oveja	la oBEcha
sheepdog	el perro pastor	el PErrro passTOR
sheet	la sábana	la SSAbana
shell	la concha	la KONtsha
shellfish	los mariscos	loss maREEsskoss
to shine	brillar	breelYAR
ship	el barco	el BARko
shirt	la camisa	la kaMEEssa
shoes	los zapatos	loss thaPAtoss
running shoes	los zapatos de corredor	loss thaPAtoss de korrreDOR
shops	las tiendas	lass TYENdas
shop assistant (m)	el dependiente	el depenDYENte
shop assistant (f)	la dependienta	la depenDYENta
shopkeeper (m)	el tendero	el tenDEro
shopkeeper (f)	la tendera	la tenDEra
shop window	el escaparate	el eskapaRAte
to shop at the market	hacer las compras	aTHER lass KOMprass
to go shopping	ir de tiendas	eer de TYENdass
shopping bag	la bolsa de compras	la BOLssa de KOMprass
shopping cart	la carretilla	la karrreTEElya
short	corto(a)	KORto(a)
to be short	ser bajo(a)	sser BAcho(a)
shoulder	el hombro	el OMbro
to shout	gritar	greeTAR
shower	la ducha	la DOOTsha
to have a shower	ducharse	dootSHARsse
with shower	con ducha	kon DOOTsha
shut	cerrado(a)	theRRRAdo(a)
shy	retraído(a)	rrretraEEdo(a)
to be sick, vomit	vomitar	bomeeTAR
side	el lado	el LAdo
to sightsee	visitar los lugares de interés	beesseeTAR loss looGAress de eenteRESS
signpost	el poste indicador	el POsste eendeekaDOR
silly	tonto(a)	TONto(a)
silver	la plata	la PLAta
made of silver	de plata	de PLAta
to sing	cantar	kanTAR
to sing out of tune	cantar desafinado	kanTAR dessafeeNAdo
singer (m/f)	el/la cantante	el/la kanTANte

English	Spanish	Pronunciation
single room	la habitación individual	la abeetaTHYONN eendeebee-DWAL
sink	el fregadero	el fregaDEro
sister	la hermana	la erMAna
to sit by the fire	sentarse al fuego	ssenTARsse al FWEgo
to sit down	sentarse	ssenTARsse
to be sitting down	estar sentado(a)	essTAR ssenTAdo(a)
six	seis	sseyss
sixteen	dieciséis	deeyetheeSEYSS
sixty	sesenta	sseSSENta
size	el tamaño	el taMANyo
What size is this?	¿Qué tamaño es esto?	ke taMANyo ess ESSto
skis	los esquís	loss essKEES
ski boots	las botas de esquí	lass BOtass de essKEE
ski instructor (m)	el instructor de esquí	el eensstrookTOR de essKEE
ski instructor (f)	la instructora de esquí	la eensstrookTOra de essKEE
ski pole	el bastón de esquí	el bassTONN de essKEE
ski resort	el centro de esquí	el THENtro de essKEE
ski slope, ski run	la pista	la PEEssta
to go skiing	esquiar	esskeeAR
skillful, good with your hands	hábil	Abeel
skin	la piel	la pyel
skirt	la falda	la FALda
sky	el cielo	el THYElo
skyscraper	el rascacielos	el rraskaTHYEloss
to sleep	dormir	dorMEER
Sleep well.	¡Que duermas bien!	ke DWERmass byen
sleeping-car	el coche-cama	el kotshe-KAma
sleeping bag	el saco de dormir	el SAko de dorMEER
to be sleepy	estar cansado(a)	essTAR kanSSAdo(a)
slide	el tobogán	el toboGANN
slim	delgado(a)	delGAdo(a)
to slip	resbalar	rrezbaLAR
slippers	las zapatillas	thapaTEELyas
slope	la cuesta	la KWEsta
slow	lento(a)	LENto(a)
to slow down	reducir la velocidad	rredooTHEER la belotheeDATH
to smell sweet	oler bien	oLER BYEN
small	pequeño(a)	peKENyo(a)
to smile	sonreír	ssonreEER
smoke	el humo	el OOmo
smoke stack (ship)	la chimenea	la tsheemeNEa
snake	la serpiente	la sserPYENte
to sneeze	estornudar	esstornooDAR
to snore	roncar	rronKAR
snow	la nieve	la NYEbe
It's snowing.	Nieva.	NYEba
snowman	el hombre de nieve	el OMbre de NYEbe
soaked to the skin	estar calado(a)	essTAR kaLAdo(a)
soap	el jabón	el chaBONN
soccer ball	el balón	el baLONN
to play soccer	jugar al fútbol	chooGAR al FOODbol
society	la sociedad	la ssotheeyeDATH
socks	los calcetines	loss kaltheTEEness
sofa	el sofá	el ssoFA
soft (smooth to the touch)	suave	SSWAbe
soft (opposite of hard)	blando(a)	BLANdo(a)
soil	la tierra	la TYErrra
soldier	el soldado	el ssolDAdo
someone	alguien	ALgeeyen
son	el hijo	el EEcho
only son	el hijo único	el EEcho OOneeko
to sort, to sort out, to arrange	ordenar	ordeNAR
soup	la sopa	la SSOpa
south	el sur	el ssoor
South Pole	el polo sur	el POlo ssoor
to sow	sembrar	ssemBRAR
space	el espacio	el essPAtheeyo
spaceship	la nave espacial	la NAbe esspaTHYAL
spade	la pala	la PAla
Spain	España	essPANya
Spanish (language or subject)	el español	el esspanYOL
sparrow	el gorrión	el gorrreeYONN
spelling	la ortografía	la ortografEEya
to spend money	gastar dinero	gasTAR deeNEro
spider	la araña	la aRANya
spinach	las espinacas	lass esspeeNAkass
to splash	salpicar	salpeeKAR
spoon	la cuchara	la kootSHAra
sport	el deporte	el dePORte
sports equipment	equipo de deporte (m)	eKEEpo de dePORte
sports field	el campo de fútbol	el kAMpo de FOODbol
spotlight	el foco	el FOko
spotted	con lunares	con looNAress
to sprain your wrist	dislocarse la muñeca	deezloKARsse la mooNYEka
spring	la primavera	la preemaBEra
square (shape)	el cuadrado	el kwaDRAdo
square (in a town)	la plaza	la PLAta
to play squash	jugar al scuach	chooGAR al essKWATsh
squirrel	la ardilla	la arDEELya
stable	la cuadra	la KWAdra
stage (theatre)	la escena	la essTHEna
staircase, stairs	la escalera	la esskaLEra
stamp	el sello	el SSELyo
to stand up	ponerse de pie	poNErsse de pye
to be standing	estar de pie	essTAR de pye
star	la estrella	la essTRELya
to start off	arrancar	arrranKAR
starter (meal)	para empezar	PAra empeZAR
station	la estación	la esstaTHYON
statue	la estatua	la essTAtooa
to stay in a hotel	quedar en un hotel	keDAR en oon oTEL
steak	el filete	el feeLEte
to steal	robar	rroBAR
steep	empinado(a)	empeeNAdo(a)
steering wheel	el volante	el boLANte
stewardess	la azafata	la athaFAta
to stick	pegar	peGAR
to sting	picar	peeKAR
stomach	el estómago	el essTOmago
to have stomach ache	tener dolor de estómago	teNER doLOR de essTOmago

storm	la tormenta	la torMENta
story	el cuento	el KWENto
straight (for hair)	laso(a)	LAsso(a)
straight hair	el pelo laso	el PElo LAsso
to go straight on	seguir todo derecho	sseGEER TOdo deRETsho
strawberry	la fresa	la FREssa
stream	el arroyo	el aRRROyo
street	la calle	la KALye
street light	el poste de la luz	el POSSte de la LOOTH
street market	el mercado abierto	el merKAdo abYErto
side street	la bocacalle	la bokaKAl ye
one way street	dirección única	deerekTHYONN OOneeka
to stretch	estirar	essteeRAR
stretcher	la camilla	la kaMEELya
striped	a rayas	a RRAyass
stroller	el cochecito de ninõs	el kotsheTHEEto de NEENyoss
strong	fuerte	FWERte
student (m/f)	el/la estudiante	el/la esstooDYANte
to study	estudiar	esstoodeeYAR
subject (of study)	la asignatura	la asseegnaTOOra
to subtract	restar	rrressTAR
suburb	las afueras	lass aFWErass
subway	el cruce subterrráneo	el KROOthe soobteRRAneo
subway	el metro	el MEtro
subway station	la estación de metro	la esstaTHYONN de MEtro
sugar	el azúcar	el aTHOOkar
suitcase	la maleta	la maLEta
summer	el verano	el beRAno
summit	la cima	la THEEma
sun	el sol	el ssol
The sun is shining.	Brilla el sol.	BREELya el ssol
to sunbathe	tomar un baño de sol	toMAR oon BANyo de ssol
Sunday	domingo (m)	doMEENGgo
sunglasses	las gafas de sol	lass GAfass de ssol
sunrise	la salida del sol	la ssaLEEda del ssol
sunset	la puesta del sol	la PWESSta de ssol
sunshade	el parasol	el paraSSOL
suntan lotion (or oil)	el aceite para el sol	el aTHEYte PAra el ssol
supermarket	el supermercado	el ssoopermerKAdo
to go to the supermarket	ir al supermercado	eer al ssoopermerKAdo
surgeon (m/f)	el cirujano	el theerooCHAno
surname	el apellido	el apelYEEdo
to sweat	sudar	ssooDAR
sweater	el jersey	el cherSSEY
sweet, charming	encantador(a)	enkantaDOR(a)
sweet (sugary)	dulce	DOOLthe
to swim, to have a swim	nadar	naDAR
swimming pool	la piscina	la peessTHEEna
swing	el columpio	el koLOOMpeeyo
to switch the light off	apagar	apaGAR
to switch the light on	encender la luz	enthenDER la looth
Switzerland	Suiza	SSWEEtha

T

table	la mesa	la MEssa
bedside table	la mesilla de noche	la meSSEELya de NOTshe
to set the table	poner la mesa	poNER la MEssa
tablecloth	el mantel	el manTEL
tail	el rabo	el RRAbo
to take	tomar	toMAR
to take the bus	coger el bus	koCHER el booss
to take an exam	examinarse	essameeNARsse
to take a photograph	tomar una foto	toMAR OOna FOto
to take someone's pulse	tomar el pulso	toMAR el POOLsso
to take someone's temperature	tomar la temperatura	toMAR la temperaTOOra
to take off	despegar	desspeGAR
to take out, to draw	sacar	ssaKAR
to take money out	sacar dinero del banco	ssaKAR deeNEro del BANGko
to be tall	ser alto(a)	sser ALto(a)
tame	manso(a)	MANsso(a)
tanned	bronceado(a)	brontheAdo(a)
tap	el grifo	el GREEfo
to tap your feet	zapatear	THApatear
tart	la tarta	la TARta
taste, flavor	el sabor	el ssaBOR
to taste, to try	probar	proBAR
It tastes good.	Está muy rico.	essTA mooy RRREEko
taxes	los impuestos	loss eemPWESStoss
taxi	el taxi	el TAKssee
to hail a taxi	parar un taxi	paRAr oon TAKssee
taxi-driver	el taxista	el takSSEESSta
taxi stand	la parada de taxis	la paRAda de TAKsseess
tea	el té	el te
tea towel	el paño de cocina	el PANyo de koTHEEna
to teach	enseñar	enssenYAR
teacher (m)	el profesor	el profeSSOR
teacher (f)	la profesora	la profeSSOra
team	el equipo	el eKEEpo
teapot	la tetera	la teTEra
to tear	rasgar	rrrazGAR
telegram	el telegrama	el teleGRAma
telephone	el teléfono	el teLEfono
telephone area code	la cifra regional	la THEEfra rrecheeoNAL
telephone box	la cabina de teléfono	la kaBEEna de teLEfono
telephone directory	la guía de teléfonos	la GEEya de teLEfonoss
telephone number	el número de teléfono	el NOOmero de teLEfono
to answer the telephone	contestar al teléfono	kontessTAR el teLEfono
to make a phone call, to dial	hacer una llamada	aTHER OOna Lyamada
telescope	el telescopio	el telessKOpeeyo
television	la televisión	la telebeeSSYON
to have a temperature	tener fiebre	teNER FYEbre
to take someone's temperature	tomar la temperatura	toMAR la temperaTOOra

English	Spanish	Pronunciation
ten	diez	deeYETH
tenant, lodger (m/f)	el/la huésped	el/la ooESSpeth
tennis	el tenis	el TEneess
tennis court	la pista de tenis	la PEESSta de TEneess
tennis player (m/f)	el/la tenista	el/la teNEESSta
to play tennis	jugar al tenis	chooGAR al TEneess
tent	la tienda de campaña	la TYENda de kamPANya
to thank	dar las gracias	dar lass GRAtheeass
Thank you for your letter of...	Gracias por su carta del...	GRAtheeyass por ssoo KARta del
Thank you very much.	¡Muchas gracias!	MOOTshass GRAtheeyass
That will be... (cost)	Todo es...	TOdo ess
to thaw	deshelar	desseLAR
theatre	el teatro	el teAtro
then, at that time	entonces	enTONthess
thermometer	el termómetro	el terMOmetro
thin	flaco(a)	FLAKo(a)
a third	una tercera parte	OOna terTHEra PARte
the third (for dates only)	el tres	el tress
thirteen	trece	TREthe
thirty	treinta	TREeenta
to be thirsty	tener sed	teNER sseth
this evening	esta tarde	ESSta TARde
this morning	esta mañana	ESSta manYAna
a thousand	mil	meel
thread	el hilo	el EElo
three	tres	tress
three quarters	tres cuartos	tress KWARtoss
The Three Wise Men	los Reyes Magos	loss RRREyess MAgoss
through	por	por
to throw	tirar	teeRAR
thrush	el zorzal	el thorTHAL
thumb	el pulgar	el poolGAR
thunder	los truenos	loss trooWEnoss
Thursday	jueves (m)	CHWEbess
ticket	el billete	el beelYEte
platform ticket	el billete de andén	el beelYEte de anDENN
return ticket	el billete de ida y vuelta	el beelYEte de EEda ee BWELta
season ticket	el billete de abono	el beelYEte de aBOno
ticket collector	el revisor	el rrrebeeSSOR
ticket machine	la máquina de billetes	la MAkeena de beelYEtess
ticket office	la taquilla	la taKEELya
to tidy up	poner orden	poNER ORden
tie	la corbata	la korBAta
tiger	el tigre	el TEEgre
tight	apretado(a)	apreTAdo(a)
tights	el leotardo	el leoTARdo
time	el tiempo	el TYEMpo
on time	llegar a la hora	lyeGAR a la Ora
to be on time	llegar a tiempo	lyeGAR a TYEMpo
What time is it?	¿Qué hora es?	ke Ora ess
times (math)	por	por
timetable	el horario	el ORAreeo
tiny	diminuto(a)	deemeeNOOto(a)
tip	la propina	la proPEEna
tire	el neumático	el neooMAteeko

English	Spanish	Pronunciation
to have a flat tire	tener una rueda deshinchada	teNErOOnaRWEda desseenTSHAda
to, towards	hacia	Atheeya
toboggan	el tobogán	el toboGANN
today	hoy	Oy
toe	el dedo de los pies	el DEdo de loss pyess
together	juntos(as)	CHOONtoss(ass)
toilet	el retrete	el rreTREte
tomato	el tomate	el toMAte
tomorrow	mañana	manYAna
tomorrow afternoon/ evening	mañana por la tarde	manYAna por la TARde
tomorrow morning	mañana por la mañana	manYAna por la manYAna
tongue	la lengua	la LENgwa
tooth	el diente	el DYENte
to have toothache	tener dolor de muelas	teNEr doLOR de MWElass
toothbrush	el cepillo de dientes	el thePEELyo de DYENtess
toothpaste	la pasta de dientes	la PASSta de DYENtess
to touch	tocar	toKAR
tour bus	el autocar	el aootoKAR
tourist (m/f)	el/la turista	el/la tooREESSta
towel	la toalla	la toALya
town	la ciudad	la theeooDATH
town hall	el ayuntamiento	el ayoontaMYENto
town square	el centro	el THENtro
toy	el juguete	el chooGEte
track	la vía	la BEEya
tracksuit	el traje de entrenamiento	el TRAche de entrenaMYENto
tractor	el tractor	el trakTOR
trade union	el sindicato	el sseendeeKAto
traffic	el tráfico	el TRAfeeko
traffic jam	el embotellamiento	el embotelya-MYENto
traffic lights	las luces de tráfico	las LOOthess de TRAfeeko
train	el tren	el tren
The train from...	El tren desde...	el tren DEZde
The train to...	El tren para...	el tren PAra
freight train	el tren de mercancías	el tren de merkanTHEEyass
inter-city train	el tren TALGO	el tren TALGO
trash can	la papelera de calle	la papeLEra de KALye
to travel by boat, to sail	ir en barco	eer en BARko
traveller (m)	el viajero	el beeaCHEro
traveller (f)	la viajera	la beeaCHEra
tray	la bandeja	a banDEcha
tree	el árbol	el ARbol
triangle	el triángulo	el treeANgoolo
trousers	los pantalones	loss pantaLOness
trowel	el desplantador	el dessplantaDOR
truck	el camión	el kamYONN
truck driver	el camionero	el kameeoNEro
true	verdadero(a)	berdaDEro(a)
trumpet	la trompeta	la tromPEta
to play the trumpet	tocar la trompeta	toKAR la tromPEta
trunk (of car)	el maletero	el maleTEro
trunk (elephant's)	la trompa	la TROMpa
T-shirt	la camiseta	la kameeSSEta
Tuesday	martes (m)	MARtess

English	Spanish	Pronunciation
Tuesday the second of June	martes, dos de junio	MARtess, doss de CHOOneeyo
tulip	el tulipán	el tooleePAN
tune	la melodía	la meloDEEya
to turn	torcer	torTHER
to turn left	torcer a la izquierda	torTHER a la eethKYErda
to turn right	torcer a la derecha	torTHER a la deRETsha
turtle	la tortuga	la torTOOga
tusk	el colmillo	el kolMEELyo
twelve	doce	DOthe
twenty	veinte	BEYeente
twin brothers (or twin brother and sister)	los gemelos	loss cheMEloss
twin sisters	las gemelas	las cheMElass
two	dos	doss

U

English	Spanish	Pronunciation
umbrella	el paraguas	el paRAgwass
uncle	el tío	el TEEyo
under	debajo de	deBAcho de
underpants	los calzoncillos	loss kalthonTHEELyoss
undershirt	la camiseta	la kameeSSETA
to get undressed	quitarse la ropa	keeTARsse la RRROpa
unemployment	el paro	el PAro
United States	los Estados Unidos	loss essTAdoss ooNEEdoss
universe	el universo	el ooneeBERsso
to unload	descargar	desskarGAR
up	arriba	aRRREEba
to get up	levantarse	lebanTARsse
upstairs	arriba	aRRREEba
to go upstairs	subir	sssooBEER
Urgent message stop phone home stop	Recado urgente stop telefonea a casa	rrreKAdo oorCHENte essTOP telefoNEA a KAssa
useful	útil	OOteel
usherette	la acomodadora	la akomodaDOra

V

English	Spanish	Pronunciation
vacation	las vacaciones	lass bakaTHYoness
to go on vacation	ir de vacaciones	eer de bakaTHYoness
to vacuum	pasar la aspiradora	paSSAR la asspeeraDOra
valley	el valle	el BALye
van	la furgoneta	la foorgoNEta
VCR (video cassette recorder)	el vídeo	el BEEdeo
veal	la ternera	la terNEra
vegetable patch	la parcela de verduras	la parTHEla de berDOOrass
vegetables	las verduras	lass berDOOrass
very well, thank you. (Answer to "How are you?")	Muy bien, ¡gracias!	mooy byen GRAtheeyass
vicar	el párroco	el PArrroko

English	Spanish	Pronunciation
video camera	la máquina de vídeo	la MAkeena de BEEdeo
view	la vista	la BEEsta
village	el pueblo	el PWEblo
vine	la vid	la beeth
vinegar	el vinagre	el beeNAgre
vineyard	la viña	la BEENya
violin	el violín	el beeoLEEN
to play the violin	tocar el violín	toKAR el beeoLEEN
volume	el volúmen	el boLOOmen
vomit	vomitar	bomeeTAR
to vote	votar	boTAR

W

English	Spanish	Pronunciation
to wag its tail	mover el rabo	moBER el RRRAbo
wages	el salario	el ssaLAreeyo
to wait for	esperar	essperRAR
waiter	el camarero	el kamaREro
waiting-room	la sala de espera	la SSAla de essPEra
to wake up	despertarse	dessperTARsse
walk	el paseo	el paSSEo
to go for a walk	dar un paseo	dar oon paSSEo
to walk, to go on foot	ir a pie	eer a pye
to walk barefoot	andar descalzo(a)	anDAR dessKALtho(a)
to take the dog for a walk	sacar el perro a paseo	saKAR el PErrro a paSSEO
wall	la pared	la paRETH
wall-to-wall carpet	la moqueta	la moKEta
wallet	la cartera	la karTEra
to wash oneself, to have a wash	lavarse	laBARsse
to wash your hair	lavarse el pelo	laBARsse el PElo
washcloth	el paño de la cara	el PANyo de la KAra
the washing	la ropa	la RRROpa
washing machine	la lavadora	la labaDOra
to do the washing	lavar la ropa	laBAR la RROpa
wasp	la avispa	la aBEESSpa
waste basket	la lata de la basura	la LAta de la baSSOOra
to watch television	ver/mirar la televisión	ber/meeRAR la telebeeSSYONN
watch	el reloj de pulsera	el rrreLOCH de poolSSEra
water	el agua (f)	el Agwa
mineral water	el agua (f) mineral	el Agwa meeneRAL
watering can	la regadera	la rrregaDEra
to waterski	hacer esquí acuático	aTHER essKEE aKWAteeko
wave	la ola	la Ola
way, path	el camino	el kaMEEno
to ask the way	preguntar el camino	pregoonTAR el kaMEEno
Which way is...?	¿Por dónde está...?	por DONde essTA
weak	débil	DEbeel
to wear	llevar	lyeBAR
to wear glasses	llevar gafas	lyeBAR GAfass
weather	el tiempo	el TYEMpo
weather forecast	el pronóstico del tiempo	el proNOSSteeko del TYEMpo
What is the weather like?	¿Qué tiempo hace?	ke TYEMpo Athe
wedding	la boda	la BOda
wedding ring	el anillo	el aNEELyo

Wednesday	miércoles (m)	MYERkoless
weed	el hierbajo	el yerBAcho
to weed	quitar los hierbajos	keeTAR loss yerBAchoss
week	la semana	la sseMAna
week-end	el fin de semana	el feen de sseMAna
weeping willow	el sauce (llorón)	el SAOOthe (lyoRONN)
to weigh	pesar	peSSAR
to weigh yourself	pesarse	peSSARsse
weight	el peso	el PEsso
well	bien	byen
to have eaten well	haber comido bien	aBER koMEEdo byen
Very well, thank you. (answer to "How are you?")	Muy bien, ¡gracias!	mooy byen GRAtheeyass
west	el oeste	el oESSte
West Germany	República Federal Alemana (/RFA)	la rrrePOOBleeka fedeRAL aleMANa/errre-efe-a
What is the weather like?	¿Qué tiempo hace?	ke TYEMpo Athe
What size is this?	¿Qué tamaño es esto?	ke taMANyo ess ESSto
What time is it?	¿Qué hora es?	ke Ora ess
What's your name?	Cómo te llamas?	KOmo te lyamass
What would you like?	¿Qué van a tomar?	ke ban a toMAR
wheat	el trigo	el TREEgo
wheel	la rueda	la RWEda
wheelbarrow	la carretilla	la karrreTEELya
Which way is...?	¿Por dónde está...?	por DONde essTA
to whisper	cuchichear	kootsheetsheAR
white	blando(a)	BLANdo(a)
Who's speaking? (on telephone)	¿Quién habla?	kyen Abla
width	el ancho	el ANTsho
wife	la mujer	la mooCHER
wild	salvaje	ssalBAche
wild flowers	las flores del campo	lass FLOress del KAMpo
to win	ganar	gaNAR
wind	el viento	el BYENto
window	la ventana	la benTAna
to go window-shopping	ir de escaparates	eer de esskapaRAtess
window display, shop window	el escaparate	el esskapaRAte
windshield	el parabrisas	el paraBREESSas
to windsurf	hacer tabla hawaiana	aTHER TAbla chawaYAna
It's windy.	Hace viento.	Athe BYENto
wine	el vino	el BEEno
wing	el ala	el Ala
winter	el invierno	el eenBYerno
with	con	kon
with balcony	con balcón	kon balKONN
with shower	con ducha	kon DOOTsha
without	sin	sseen
woman	la mujer	la mooCHER
wood	el bosque	el BOSSke
wooden, made of wood	de madera	de maDEra
woodwork	la carpintería	la karpeenteREEya
woollen	de lana	de LAna
word	la palabra	la paLAbra
to work	trabajar	trabaCHAR
to go to work	ir a trabajar	eer a trabaCHAR
world	el mundo	el MOONdo
I would like...	Querriá...	keRRREEya
wrapping	la envoltura	la enbolTOOra
to write	escribir	esskreeBEER
to write a check	hacer un cheque	aTHER oon TSHEke
to write a letter	escribir una carta	esskreeBEER OOna KARta
wrist	la muñeca	la moonYEka
writing paper	el papel de cartas	el paPEL de KARtass

Y

yarn	la lana	la LAna
to yawn	bostezar	bossteTHAR
year	el año	el ANyo
yellow	amarillo(a)	amaREELyo(a)
yes	si	ssee
yesterday	ayer	aYER
yesterday evening	anoche	aNOTshe
yesterday morning	ayer por la mañana	aYER por la manYAna
yogurt	el yogur	el yoGOOR
young	joven	CHOben
young, little	pequeño(a)	peKENyo(a)
younger than	más pequeño(a) que	mass peKENyo(a) ke
Yours faithfully,	Le saluda atentamente,	le ssaLOOda atentaMENte

Z

zebra	la cebra	la THEbra
zero	cero	THEro
zip code	el distrito postal	el deessTREEto possTAL
zipper	la cremallera	la kremalyera
zoo	el zoológico	el tho-oLOcheeko
zoo keeper	el guardián de zoo	el gwardeeYAN de tho-o

First published in 1988 by Usborne Publishing Ltd
Usborne House, 83-85 Saffron Hill
London EC1N 8RT, England.
Copyright © 1988 Usborne Publishing Ltd.

The name Usborne and the device 🐻 are Trade Marks of Usborne Publishing Ltd.

All rights reserved. No part of this publication may be reproduced, stored in a retrieval system or transmitted by any form or by any means mechanical, electronic, photocopying, recording, or otherwise, without the prior permission of the publisher.

Printed in Great Britain.

AE